EDITED BY
COLIN MCDOUGALL
GEORGE KENDALL
WENDY CHAMBERLAIN MP

THE FUTURE OF
SOCIAL DEMOCRACY

Essays to Mark the 40th Anniversary of the
Limehouse Declaration

First published in Great Britain in 2021 by

Policy Press, an imprint of
Bristol University Press
University of Bristol
1–9 Old Park Hill
Bristol
BS2 8BB
UK
t: +44 (0)117 954 5940
e: bup-info@bristol.ac.uk

Details of international sales and distribution partners are available at
policy.bristoluniversitypress.co.uk

British Library Cataloguing in Publication Data
A catalogue record for this book is available from the British Library

ISBN 978-1-4473-6126-8 paperback
ISBN 978-1-4473-6127-5 ePub
ISBN 978-1-4473-6128-2 ePdf

Cover design: Clifford Hayes
Front cover image: ARROW DOOR
Bristol University Press and Policy Press use environmentally
responsible print partners.
Printed in Great Britain by CMP, Poole

This book is dedicated to Roy Jenkins, Shirley Williams and Bill Rogers, founders of the Social Democratic Party (SDP), who came with the party to form the Liberal Democrats.

Contents

Notes on the authors

Vince Cable was leader of the Liberal Democrats from 2017 to 2019. He stood for Parliament as a member of the SDP and was elected as Liberal Democrat Member of Parliament (MP) for Twickenham in 1997. He has been the party's Deputy Leader, Treasury Spokesperson, then Secretary of State for Business, Innovation and Skills in the Coalition government (2010–15). He has a professional background as an economist.

Wendy Chamberlain is MP for North East Fife, the Liberal Democrats' Chief Whip in the House of Commons and Spokesperson for Work and Pensions, and also for Scotland and Wales. She has served 12 years as a police officer and joined the Liberal Democrats in 2015.

Chris Huhne is an energy and climate change consultant. He stood for Parliament as a member of the SDP, becoming a Liberal Democrat Member of the European Parliament (MEP), MP and then Secretary of State for Energy and Climate Change in the Coalition government (2010–12). He has a professional background in journalism and the City.

Ian Kearns is Director of the Social Liberal Forum. He has worked as Deputy Director of the Institute for Public Policy Research (IPPR) and co-founded the European Leadership Network. He has written for *The Guardian*, *The Times* and many other major media outlets. He joined the Liberal Democrats from Labour in 2018.

George Kendall is Chair of the Social Democrat Group. He joined the Liberal Democrats from the SDP. He has since served as a councillor and a Liberal Democrat campaigns officer. He has a professional background in software development.

Roger Liddle is a Labour peer, chair of the Policy Network, county councillor and Pro-Chancellor of the University of Lancaster. While in the SDP, he served on its National Policy Committee. After returning to Labour, he was Special Advisor on European Matters to Tony Blair and Principal Advisor to the President of the European Commission.

Colin McDougall is Secretary of the Social Democrat Group. He is also the Liberal Democrat Campaigns Officer for the South Central Region. He has a professional background in project management. He joined the Liberal Democrats from Labour in 2017.

Dick Newby is Leader of the Liberal Democrats in the House of Lords. He was National Secretary of the SDP. In the Liberal Democrats, he was Charles Kennedy's Chief of Staff from 1999 to 2006. While in the Lords, he has also served as Chief Whip and Treasury Spokesperson. He has a professional background as a director, a consultant and in charity work.

Sarah Olney is MP for Richmond Park and the Liberal Democrats' Spokesperson on Transport, Business and Industrial Strategy, and Energy and Climate Change. She has previously served as the party's Spokesperson for International Trade and Education. She has a professional background in accountancy.

Julie Smith is the Liberal Democrats' Defence Spokesperson in the House of Lords. She joined the Liberal Democrats from the SDP. She has served as a councillor and as Vice Chair of the Liberal Democrats' Policy Committee. She is a Cambridge University academic, specialising in European politics.

Stephen Williams is the Liberal Democrats' candidate for Mayor of the West of England. He joined the Liberal Democrats from the SDP. He has served as a county and city councillor. While MP for Bristol West, he was Liberal Democrat Shadow Minister for Schools, and a minister in the Department for Communities and Local Government. He was the only member of the Coalition government to have been on free school meals as a child.

Foreword

Colin McDougall, George Kendall and Wendy Chamberlain MP

This book is written to grapple with the serious challenges the country faces in the coming decades and is inspired by the example of those who wrote the Limehouse Declaration 40 years ago. We have invited contributors to reflect on these challenges, and to propose realistic solutions. We have also encouraged them to think boldly and feel free to disagree with each other.

January 2021 marks the 40th anniversary of the Limehouse Declaration and the launch of the Social Democratic Party (SDP) that followed. Through the 1980s, the SDP offered the most coherent ideas to challenge Thatcherism; these became the intellectual bedrock for the best of New Labour. They were also central to the ethos of the Liberal Democrats, which was formed from a merger of the SDP and the Liberals.

The Social Democrat Group was formed in 2015 to promote this social democratic heritage within the Liberal Democrats and to build on these ideas to address the challenges of the future. These include appalling levels of poverty, the aftermath of our exit from the European Union (EU) and the rise of populists, who fill digital platforms with intolerance and have an increasing voice in mainstream media.

This collection of essays is an important part of that ongoing work. We are enormously grateful to the leading politicians who have produced the excellent essays that make up this book.

While the Social Democrat Group is a Liberal Democrat group, there are many social democrats in other parties and none, such as Roger Liddle, one of the contributors to this book. The group has always sought to engage with them. If this is you, this book is for you too.

The world has changed dramatically since the Limehouse Declaration set out the underlying principles of a new party. It is extraordinary to think that words written in a world with only three television channels and no smartphones, and that was closer to the Second World War than today, should be relevant today.

Social democracy has many definitions. In our view, it combines:

- a determination to pursue policies that will work;
- a commitment to fight for the vulnerable; and
- a belief that for democracy to thrive, policies must work for everyone, including the affluent.

Through this book, we seek to strengthen the voice of a political philosophy that has done more to transform the world for the better than any other in the last 100 years. In modern Britain, the National Health Service (NHS), state investment programmes and social insurance are the result of this social democratic heritage.

One of the greatest qualities of the SDP was an atmosphere of creative policy exploration, which created solutions that were not just radical, but also workable. The greatest successes of social democracy have often owed as much to building a consensus about values and policies. The technological and social change of recent decades has put huge strain on this consensus in important areas of policy, as Ian Kearns describes in Chapter Three.

Voters are rightly sceptical when social democrats propose large-scale change through an active state as they fear these changes are not based on fairness and rigorous thinking. However, when a consensus has been achieved, social democratic reforms have not just been delivered, but been accepted by all parties. This has meant that even when social democrats have lost power, the influence of their values has continued, for example, in the way all parties now support the free provision of healthcare through the NHS.

Many of the policies outlined in the following chapters would, if implemented, make huge differences to people's lives, for example, Chris Huhne's proposals for long-term policies that would increase the provision of decent housing and make it more affordable. However, as social democrats and liberals, we need to do more than propose policies; we need to win public support.

This is a considerable challenge for all ambitious policies. For example, many in the centre-left have argued for a universal basic income. The Social Democrat Group has a range of opinions on this issue, as do the contributors to this book. The policy seeks to resolve, or at least mitigate, many of our social ills, including job insecurity, rapid technological change and poverty. However, there is a significant challenge to convince voters that the significant rise in taxes is justified, and that it will deliver what is promised.

This is true for many other policies, including the free trade policies which Sarah Olney describes in Chapter Six, and the foreign and defense policies which Julie Smith describes in Chapter Seven.

A new social contract

All mature states have some kind of social contract to create a stable consensus, where individuals give power to the state, for example, to levy taxes, in exchange for certain benefits. In some countries, this is defined in a written constitution; in others, like the UK, it is more implicit – but it still exists.

A substantial increase in taxes to create a more just society would change the existing implicit social contract in the UK. If we are to win public support, we need to consider what that contract would look like. The cost in increased taxes will be self-evident. To win voters over, we need to convince them that the gains are worthwhile, whether in improved pooling of risk or an improved social fabric.

The social contract also implies obligations that citizens have to wider society. For example, that if they make appointments with their doctor, they attend them. Many voters believe that the implicit contract involved in their funding the welfare state is not being kept by others. To increase funding for the welfare state, we will need to reassure these voters.

Responding to voters' concerns

The unexpected Conservative majority in December 2019 was a painful defeat for both Labour and the Liberal

Democrats. The pain of this defeat has been compounded by the fact that many of those on lower incomes, whose lives we seek to improve, switched to the Conservatives. This is a serious political failure and we need to consider why it happened. To have a chance of implementing the excellent solutions outlined in the following chapters requires us to resolve this dilemma.

The following chapters are written by experienced politicians, rather than academics, who are painfully aware of the need to reach out beyond those who think like us. On his election as Liberal Democrat leader, Ed Davey rightly emphasised the importance of listening, and not just to those who agree with us. Those of us who are activists on the centre-left should do the same.

Reaching out must be about more than policies. It may involve changing the way we express ourselves. Probably the most painful electoral defeat in the last ten years was the election of Donald Trump. On 9 September 2016, Hilary Clinton said: 'you could put half of Trump's supporters into what I call the basket of deplorables.... They're racist, sexist, homophobic, xenophobic, Islamophobic.'[1] It was a catastrophic gaffe that was used repeatedly by the Trump campaign. Not only did it energise Trump's base, but some who were still undecided thought her insult might be directed at them. She quickly apologised, but the damage was done, perhaps because those words were perceived to reflect the underlying attitude of many liberal members of the Democrats. Social democrats and liberals in the UK should consider whether we have made similar mistakes.

Engaging with these voters will sometimes require us to make compromises. Such compromises are not a betrayal of our values. Those who voted tactically for Hillary Clinton to keep out Trump in 2016, whether from the Left or the Right, were compromising, but they were also acting out of deep principle. We want voters to give us tactical support in the UK, but we will be unable to do so if we reject the idea of seeking common ground with them.

We must also be careful about making superficial judgements. Instead, we should work hard to understand what people really mean. Ian Kearns, director of our sister group, the Social Liberal Forum, has talked about an experience in Germany.[2] Locals feared the settling of angry young male refugees in their village, but when the proposal changed to settling refugee families with young children, they agreed to it. In the same way, if we meet communities in the UK who express similar concerns, we must engage with them. We certainly should not dismiss their concerns as racist.

Some of their concerns were the result of past government decisions. In 2004, Tony Blair's government decided to open its borders immediately rather than apply transitional controls. They predicted EU immigration to the UK would be between 5,000 and 13,000. In practice, the migration was far higher. By 2007, 112,000 had entered the UK from new EU member states in a single year.[3] This may have undermined the trust of many of the voters who have deserted the centre-left and who became disillusioned with the EU. However, this loss of confidence in the centre-left need not be permanent as long as we actively engage with these voters.

We should also consider the warnings of Michael Sandel[4]: by pursuing meritocracy without creating a level playing field for those without a privileged background, the liberal Left has abandoned the working class. In Chapter Eight, entitled 'How do we deliver social justice through education?', Stephen Williams proposes a series of policies to improve life chances for the disadvantaged. Sandel also calls for the redistribution of esteem, as well as money, to those doing work that does not require a degree. This cannot be done easily, and will require genuine engagement with these people.

Conclusion

Social democracy has dramatically improved the lives of people across Britain in the last century but it has lost support to populists in recent years. This collection of essays by leading social democrats and liberals aims to promote new social democratic thinking to arrest this decline.

While this will not be straightforward, we should not despair. In the 1930s, there was a fatalism among many democrats that the future belonged to fascism and communism. It did not. Nor do all the signs show that populism is on the rise. Polling shows that opposition to immigration has softened since the Brexit vote,[5] support for most forms of benefit remains high,[6] the hostility to those on benefits that existed around 2005 has subsided[7] and, within Western Europe, opposition to minority groups is low.[8]

If we learn from past mistakes, and engage with the concerns of ordinary people, the proposals in the excellent essays in this book can be delivered, and the lives of many improved.

Notes

[1] 'Mook: Clinton's "deplorables" comment "definitely could have alienated" voters', CNN, December 2016. A study showed that

Clinton's 'deplorables' comment had the greatest impact in alienating undecided voters.

[2] 'Building a "do tank" not just a think tank with Ian Kearns', LibDem Podcast, YouTube, August 2020 (23.09 minutes in).

[3] Erica Consterdine (2016) 'The huge political cost of Blair's decision to allow Eastern European migrants unfettered access to Britain', theconversation.com, November, https://theconversation.com/the-huge-political-cost-of-blairs-decision-to-allow-eastern-european-migrants-unfettered-access-to-britain-66077

[4] *The Guardian* (2020) 'Michael Sandel: "The populist backlash has been a revolt against the tyranny of merit"', September, www.theguardian.com/books/2020/sep/06/michael-sandel-the-populist-backlash-has-been-a-revolt-against-the-tyranny-of-merit

[5] There is a preference in the UK for reduced migration but it has softened since the Brexit vote. See 'UK public opinion toward immigration: overall attitudes and level of concern', https://migrationobservatory.ox.ac.uk/

[6] John Hudson and Neil Lunt, 'Winning support for the safety net' (Table 4, p 17), https://england.shelter.org.uk/__data/assets/pdf_file/0003/1359741/Winning_Support_for_the_Safety_Net_Short_Report.pdf

[7] *The Economist* (2019) 'Our attitudes to welfare have undergone a quiet revolution since Benefits Street', *The Economist*, 18 July, https://inews.co.uk/news/politics/our-attitudes-to-welfare-have-undergone-a-quiet-revolution-since-benefits-street-315596

[8] Gallup polling in 2019 showed opposition to minority groups in Europe is relatively low in Western Europe but high among supporters of radical right-wing parties. See: www.pewresearch.org/global/2019/10/14/minority-groups/

Introduction: what are the priorities for social democrats?

Vince Cable

Political parties that could be described as social democratic have been in decline for some years, particularly in the countries where they have historically been strongest: Britain, Germany and in Scandinavia. Others, which were loosely associated, outside the Western world, as in India and Brazil, have largely disappeared. Almost everywhere, competing voices – nationalism, ethnically based populism and authoritarian 'strong men' – have drowned out the appeal of social democracy and captured a substantial section of the electoral base of social democratic parties. That base was in any event contracting because of structural change in the economy away from manufacturing and unionised employment, and the greater priority for younger voters of new issues like the environment. The main appeal of social democrats – that they offer the best of capitalism and socialism, both the economic effectiveness of the former and the fairness of the latter – was increasingly seen to be not credible or relevant.

The COVID-19 pandemic may produce big and long-term changes to the scenery against which political drama is being played out. It could hasten the decline of social democracy; however, it could also help it stage a revival. Certainly, the challenges now being thrown up are those to which social democrats have produced answers in the past: mass unemployment; the re-emergence of large-scale mass poverty in the poorest countries; protectionism and lack of international cooperation; and growing dependence on the state to coordinate, plan and be the health provider, employer and safety net of last resort. Social democrats, in government and out, were key to the post-war consensus that was instrumental in tackling these problems, which have now resurfaced in a new way.

However, there are competing political models and ideas. Nationalism and populism are powerful forces in some countries (the US, Russia, China, Brazil, Mexico and India). Overlapping with those is the cult of 'the authoritarian strongman'. Then there are what can be called the 'welfare technocracies' of East Asia. There are pockets, which may grow, of aggressive and radical individualism. And, in contrast, there are strongly communitarian movements at local level: sometimes inclusive; sometimes exclusive. The issue for social democrats is whether they can offer a mixture of competence and compassion that can transcend the competition in a democratic context.

Who are the social democrats?

The social democratic tribe is a lot bigger than represented by the parties that are descended from the socialist tradition like the UK

Labour Party and its Antipodean cousins, the Social Democratic Party (SPD) in Germany, and the assorted social democrat parties around Europe. There are some social democratic parties that call themselves 'socialist', as in Spain, or 'labour', as in Norway, or 'democrat', as in Italy, and we should not include some that call themselves 'social democrat' but are rebadged 'communists'. We should include the US Democrats, who never went through a socialist phase. There are also 'social liberals' who emerged from classical liberal parties but are now largely indistinguishable from social democrats, like the Canadian Liberals (though they have competition from the New Democrats), and others like the Dutch 66, the Swedish Liberals and Macron's En Marche where there are big areas of overlap. The Liberal Democrats in the UK are such a hybrid, and the identification often has more to do with a country's voting system and its history of political schism than meaningful working definitions of social democracy.

What is striking and disappointing is that social democracy has not travelled well outside the heartland of Western Europe, North America and Australasia. In Asia, Lee's People's Action Party (PAP) in Singapore was modelled on the British Labour Party but came to despise the welfare state. On the bigger canvass of India, the Congress Party seemed to have similar values to European social democrats but succumbed to rampant corruption. The same can be said for the Brazilian Workers Party. There are recognisably social democratic parties in many places (Ghana, Jamaica, South Africa, Costa Rica, Japan, Taiwan and Korea) but national idiosyncrasies tend to outweigh what they have in common.

Those national variations stem from different histories. Some social democratic parties, as in Sweden, broke with their revolutionary socialist ancestry over a century ago and have maintained a consistently reformist and democratic personality ever since. In some cases, as in Germany, there was a moment when the party redefined itself as unambiguously social democratic – the Bad Godesberg conference in 1959 – and it has remained aloof from parties of the far Left like Die Linke.

Despite the efforts of Anthony Crosland and others to achieve a similar clarification in the UK, ambiguity remained, leading initially to the SDP breakaway. Moreover, despite the efforts of Neil Kinnock, John Smith and Tony Blair to cement the social democratic character of the Labour Party, they succeeded only temporarily, leading to the bizarre spectacle of their party being captured by revolutionary socialists. Brexit has also created new geographical and ideological wounds. In the meantime, the Liberal Democrats became the voice of many social democrats, as well as liberals, but it is marginalised by the electoral system.

This very varied, eclectic, mix of parties and political traditions makes it difficult to locate the common denominator. There is a common thread in the Rawlsian tradition of thought, which emphasises individual freedoms alongside a shared sense of fairness and that has at its heart a 'social contract'. The current crisis is also forcing social democrats to come up with new or reworked policy ideas to tackle new problems or old problems in a new guise.

What is to be done?

I see the main political challenge as to fashion what have been called 'visions to touch' as opposed to small-scale technocracy, on the one hand, and abstract slogans, on the other. I would identify four major areas where these 'visions' are required: large-scale unemployment; poverty and the interaction of tax and benefits; the workings of modern capitalism, especially in relation to data and the big data companies; and the threats to multilateralism.

Mass unemployment

The pandemic and lockdown have recreated a problem thought to have been solved except in specific areas like structural unemployment among young people in Southern Europe and underemployment in emerging economies in Africa and South Asia. The full scale of the problem is not yet clear, but when the temporary furlough schemes are phased out in the autumn, millions will be out of work in the UK.

In one respect, there has been an advance in policy thinking since the last depression in the 1930s to the extent that all major governments have accepted that they have a responsibility for maintaining adequate levels of aggregate demand through fiscal policy and/or the monetary policy of central banks. Aggressive monetary policy was used after the financial crisis and is being tried again. In addition, since the pandemic commenced, the main governments – the US, Germany, Japan, China, the UK and France – have all provided a large fiscal stimulus. To do so, they have accepted that they will incur substantially more public debt. There is an implicit acceptance that higher deficits and debt are not now an issue in the short run. That is not a worry for countries like the US and Japan, which can borrow in their own currencies, or like Germany and China, which have low initial debt levels. Many poorer and more indebted countries are more constrained. Others, like the UK, will need to set out a long-term debt financing plan to reassure their creditors. Social democrats will be needed to maintain commitment to a Keynesian approach – in a very fluid and uncertain world.

Not all unemployment can be dealt with through cheap money and fiscal stimulus. Much will be structurally caused by the disappearance of many firms and the obsolescence of specific skills. Various initiatives will be needed: cuts in employment costs by reducing employers' national insurance contributions (NICs); large-scale and sustained public works projects; and investment allowances, incentivising early investment. Some groups will find it very difficult to join or rejoin the labour force, especially young people without work experience and older workers close to retirement age. For the former, there are tested schemes offering a guarantee of post-school education, training or employment. For the latter, there is a need to ensure access to adult and continuing education, as well as retraining opportunities. The more successful schemes of the 1980s and the ideas successfully trialled in Sweden and Germany should inform policy.

The dogmas of the past have no role in an emergency of this kind and social democrats have an important role in escaping the public good–private bad or private good–public bad dialectics of the past. The approach will need to be eclectic and practical, and involve maximising the contributions of the private and public sectors. One of the legacies of the Coalition years is the Industrial Strategy, which provides a forum for public–private coordination and cooperation at a sector level to address long-term issues. That structure needs to be revived and strengthened to give focus to what would otherwise be random interventions at firm level.

Poverty, tax and benefits

The pandemic has exposed the limitations of the British welfare system after years of reform and cuts. Large numbers have fallen through the cracks; others have been forced to rely on the stringent benefits of Universal Credit and a patchwork of specific supports for disability and other needs. On the other hand, pensioners, protected by the 'triple lock' on the state pension, have been insulated from the economic effects of the crisis, as they were after the 2008/09 financial crisis.

The reforms of Beveridge (like Keynes, a liberal) provide a template for a comprehensive social safety net that social democrats have regarded as the right starting point. Recent adaptation of the post-war welfare state involved an attempt to create a form of negative income tax under Gordon Brown's tax credit system. The principle was good but it suffered from complexity and the practical problems of offsetting continuous changes in income in current highly volatile labour market conditions, with 'gig' work and numerous part-time earnings. The Coalition model was to simplify means-tested benefits in Universal Credit, which has however become discredited by cuts and delays in payment, while also lifting the income tax threshold, thereby lifting low earners out of income tax.

The new idea that is being embraced by many social democrats is universal basic income. The immediate attraction is that, in an emergency, it enables money to meet basic needs, and to provide purchasing power in the economy, to be paid to everyone (in principle) without time-consuming and discriminatory checks. At present, in the UK, millions of 'self-employed' and recently unemployed are not adequately covered. As a temporary measure, it should be tried.

However, as a permanent system, universal basic income is being promoted with evangelical fervour, which is unfortunate since its impact depends on precisely what it replaces and on the availability of some continued means-tested support in the form of housing benefit for high-rent areas. Social democrats should welcome localised universal basic income experiments and should, in the meantime, be pressing for changes to Universal Credit in order to make it significantly more generous to low-earner families, without the current delays and impediments.

The pandemic has highlighted some of the underlying injustices and inequities in society, such as between young and old, and in respect of wealth and income. One of the side effects of the necessary use of extraordinary monetary policy is to inflate the value of assets, both property and financial. These, in turn, are disproportionately held by older people. Social democrats should be making the case for more effective and tougher taxation of assets through inheritance taxes, capital gains taxes and taxes on high-value property.

Modern capitalism

In the Great Depression of the 1930s in the US, which potentially bears comparison with today, the New Deal was President Roosevelt's social democratic response. In fact, the New Deal was not, as widely believed, Keynesian in its economics. However, it did effect major changes to the conduct of business and strengthened the bargaining power of workers. A modern version of the New Deal is needed, not to destroy capitalism, but to remedy some of the most egregious abuses.

My main focus in the UK would be creating a tax and regulatory environment that favours stable, long-term commitment by investors over short-term, speculative activity. Some steps were taken in the Coalition years to change the culture – quarterly reporting is no longer required – but the problem remains. One important step would be to give long-term shareholders bigger voting rights. Another would be to shift the taxation of capital gains back to penalising short-term speculative activity.

Much has been written about the obligations of companies to stakeholders more widely than shareholders. Legislation in the UK already reflects those wider concerns. However, unless the legal primacy of shareholders is removed from companies, there will continue to be insufficient weight given to employee well-being and environmental and other societal factors. At the same time, it is important that entrepreneurs and investors of risk capital should be properly rewarded. The continued tax bias against risk capital and in favour of debt is a big disincentive – and has to be reversed.

There are now particular issues as a consequence of the big data companies that have come to dominate the world economy and exposed the weakness of national governments in respect of tax collection and competition policy. The European Commission has been the sole authority (outside China) to exercise some effective control over the monopoly power of the Internet platforms, and then only to a limited extent. One of the main casualties of Brexit has been the loss of that countervailing power. A major task of policy now is to create at national level a much more effective and aggressive Competition and Markets Authority to counter takeovers that further stifle competition, to impose strong standards to protect privacy (using the existing European rules), and to regulate abusive content.

Multilateralism

For social democrats, there is a clear understanding that many policy objectives in relation to trade and financial flows, tax avoidance, crime, defence, environmental commons and climate change, human rights, poverty, and development cannot be achieved at a national level alone, but require cooperation. One of the most alarming developments in recent years has been the weakening of support for multilateral bodies like the World Trade Organisation, the Bretton Woods institutions and United Nations (UN) agencies, which are more relevant than ever in repairing the damage wrought by the pandemic, especially in the poorest countries. The fact that Britain has walked away from the EU has damaged regional cooperation, as well as the UK itself. Britain will now have a less credible presence in global institutions but has a particular responsibility nonetheless for the climate negotiations soon to be held in Glasgow.

The Brexiteers' slogan of 'Global Britain' may or may not have been sincere or thought through. However, social democrats should adopt it and seek to make it meaningful in trade, development, environmental, human rights and other forums. Governments in the social democratic tradition in Sweden and Canada have shown that middleweight countries can have considerable influence for good. At the same time, a major project for the next generation will be to rebuild links with the EU, not necessarily through full membership, but through the kind of close association already enjoyed by neighbours who are not members.

Conclusion

Among the most significant challenges for social democrats are mass unemployment, poverty, the problems posed by big data companies and the weakening of multinational institutions caused by rising populism. Social democrats should remain committed to a Keynesian approach to economic matters, should learn from best practice in other countries and should adopt pragmatic, evidence-based policies.

The policies they should pursue include: a commitment to lifelong training and education; support for generous in-work benefits to low-earner families; making the case for taxing assets whose value has been inflated by recent monetary policies; a more effective authority to counter business takeovers that stifle competition or undermine the country's science base; and rebuilding the UK's relationships with our overseas partners to pursue policy objectives that cannot be achieved at a national level. However, social democrats will not return to power in Britain on the basis of policy ideas alone; they will have to overcome the tribal divisions of British political parties and the obstacles of the British 'first-past-the-post' voting system by means of tactical cooperation.

ONE

After the failed alternative vote referendum, how can electoral reform have a future?

Wendy Chamberlain MP

The Liberal Democrats have been arguing for electoral reform for many years, largely focused on replacing the first-past-the-post voting system for Westminster. During that time, despite progress in delivering more proportional systems for both the Welsh Senedd and the Scottish Parliament, the party and others have failed to make a compelling case for change.

Since the alternative vote (AV) referendum during the Coalition period, two further referendums have taken place: on Scottish Independence in 2014 and on leaving the EU in 2016. Putting to one side the position that AV is not in itself a proportional system, the outcomes of the following two referendums in the UK have made the case for electoral reform more pressing.

The politics of place, a key argument in support of first past the post, continues to persist. In an era of increasing identity politics, place has increasing importance to many. With COVID-19, however, the straining of centralised decision-making at Westminster, and better recognition of the powers held by the devolved administrations in Scotland, Wales and Northern Ireland, could mean electoral reform's time has come.

The outcome of the December 2019 general election delivered an 80-seat majority to Boris Johnson's government on less than 44 per cent of the vote, as well as a dominant Scottish National Party (SNP) in Scotland (where the disparity was even more stark, with the SNP gaining 80 per cent of the seats on only 45 per cent of the popular vote). The Brexit Party's biggest impact on the election was its decision to stand down in Conservative-held seats, effectively denying its supporters the opportunity to vote in support of them. The Liberal Democrats' own share of the vote increased by over 4 per cent but there was a decrease in seats to the current 11. These factors are leading to an increasing realisation within the Labour Party that it will be unable to return to government without the assistance of, and support for, a more proportional electoral system.

It is easy to forget that first past the post is not the default system in place across the UK. It ironically persists in England, where the vote to leave the EU has often been characterised as a vote by the left behind. Perhaps the perception of wasted votes making no difference in their local areas also had a part to play.

Many of the so-called 'red wall' seats that the Conservatives won in the 2019 general election had been held by Labour for decades, itself not a healthy state of affairs. Up until the outbreak of the coronavirus pandemic, the Conservative government had planned investment in a few of these seats to improve their local economies. That only when a seat changes hands or becomes marginal does it merit interest or investment shows that we have a flawed democracy that is underpinned by an unfair voting system.

The Scottish Parliament uses the additional member system (AMS), which was designed to prevent a majority for any party, though the SNP did gain a majority in 2011 nonetheless. At the time of writing, polling support for independence in Scotland suggests a similar outcome in the May 2021 elections, and continued wrangling about the future of the UK into the new decade seems likely.

Since 2007, local government elections in Scotland have been conducted using single transferable vote (STV). In Wales, the Senedd also uses AMS and they have recently made a significant step in that local authorities can move to STV for council elections if they wish. The Northern Irish Assembly is elected using STV, as is its local government.

It is striking how the Labour Party has adopted STV to fill vacancies in their National Executive Committee (NEC), a move supported by new leader Sir Keir Starmer. The cross-party proportional representation (PR) pressure group Make Votes Matter is proactively working with the internal Labour for Electoral Reform organisation to educate local Constituency Labour Parties (CLPs) in order to gain their commitment to PR. Recent polling suggests that 75 per cent of Labour members support changing the current Westminster voting system to a more proportional one.

One of the key claims of supporters of first past the post is that it prevents 'losers' (that is, the party that fails to win the most votes) from winning. However, this is simply not true: in the UK, the party with the most votes failed to win the general election in both 1951 and 1974.

In Europe, Belarus is the only other country to use first past the post to determine its governments. The Conservatives have been the clear dominant force in government; indeed, since the end of the Second World War, a Conservative has been prime minister for 45 years. This dominance is a key reason why there has been no move away from the first-past-the-post system. Indeed, when Labour came to power in 1997, there were discussions with Liberal Democrat leader Paddy Ashdown to introduce a more proportional system, which led to the Jenkins Commission recommendations, though these were not acted on.

First past the post results in a two-party system that clearly suits the two largest parties. Westminster as a building is set up as such, with government and opposition dispatch boxes distanced two sword widths apart in the two-sided chamber. As has become increasingly obvious over the course of the COVID-19 pandemic, first past the post does not create an effective political culture. It offers no answer to the age-old problem of the persistent minority. In an increasingly diverse country, binary options are no longer satisfactory, and the damage that binary decision-making causes can be clearly seen via recent referendums.

The problem is about to be compounded in local government in England. The Conservatives' plans to consolidate district and county councils into unitary authorities will result in fewer people being represented by anyone they voted for, which will only increase the democratic deficit in England. The restrictions being placed on the redrawing of the current parliamentary constituencies will only exacerbate this deficit further.

A political party that is out of power, such as Labour now finds itself, may well support reform to the voting system. However, the moment it wins an election and starts governing, it becomes a beneficiary of first past the post by default. No majority government of the UK has ever won more than 50 per cent of the popular vote. The SNP continually argues that Scotland does not get the government that it votes for but the harsh reality is that no one does.

So, the decision by a party in power to switch to a proportional system would mean their majority would evaporate, and would also mean a complete overhaul of the prevailing political culture. The fallout from coalition for the Liberal Democrats has meant that, since 2015, the party has explicitly ruled out a coalition agreement with either of the two main parties. However, in a proportional system, coalitions are likely to be the common form of government, and so will be something that both parties and the electorate will need to acclimatise to. This would be a good thing as it would lead to a less divisive form of politics in which all voters have an equal say at election time.

The unfairness of first past the post is often highlighted immediately after an election, but after the dust has settled, does electoral reform remain a voter priority? Those advocating for electoral reform need to make the case and demonstrate the practical benefits that fairer voting will bring to the day-to-day issues that drive voter concerns.

So, if a party in government is committed to electoral reform, what is the best way to deliver it? Clearly, they need to ensure support within their own parliamentary party. There is a vested interest for a sitting MP who wishes to be re-elected to keep the current system. However, PR does not mean the end to a sitting MP's career. An STV system using multi-member constituencies still allows MPs to represent a defined area, as well as ensuring representation for those who voted for other parties. The politics of place can be delivered by PR too.

A determined form of PR also needs to be agreed. The Make Votes Matter Good Systems agreement, supported by a number of political parties, including the Liberal Democrats, Alliance, the Green Party, SNP and Plaid Cymru, outlined the key principles of any proportional system:

- proportionality
- representation
- equal votes
- local links
- diversity
- voter choice
- accountability
- balance of stability and flexibility
- sustainability and adaptability
- voting simplicity

None of these principles would prevent a system other than STV (the Liberal Democrats' preferred system). This could mean that other options, such as Roy Jenkins's AV+ system, might come into contention, despite it not being utilised by any existing legislature. Given the prevalence of the AMS systems in the Scottish Parliament and Welsh Senedd, and STV at a local government level, it is clear that a variety of options exist, and increased voter familiarity with such systems can only be a good thing.

A path to delivering such change is clearly via another coalition, or at the very least a confidence-and-supply agreement with a commitment to real fair voting. This is a road that the party has been down before, and the resulting referendum and subsequent general election were devastating. The impact of coalition remains in the current diminished parliamentary party.

Once you have got to the point of coalition or confidence and supply, there is the question of a referendum. Given the UK's recent history, is this the right approach? Is a referendum not exactly the sort of binary politics that we want to leave in the past, along with the binary first-past-the-post system? Also, how is there any way to guarantee that any campaign will be free from misinformation? The campaign against AV ran on a 'cost of politics' basis just a year after the expenses scandal. What should have been an argument for reform was portrayed as the voice of the elites. It is important that any subsequent campaigning on the issue is seen as anything but.

It is worth considering New Zealand when looking at a path to a proportional voting system. There, it took two elections – in 1978 and 1981, where the Labour Party won the most votes but the National Party took more seats and went on to form the government. The closeness of time between these results was a contributory factor that catalysed public opinion. It became clear to voters that the system was delivering an unfair result, where the 'losers' were rewarded with government.

This realisation was what brought about the commitment to change the voting system, much like the journey that Labour in the UK is currently on now. When Labour in New Zealand won in 1984, they promised a Royal Commission. The commission went on to recommend a mixed-member proportional system.

However, even in New Zealand, there were obstacles. Neither the Labour Party nor the National Party was keen to implement the Royal Commission's findings. Each party eventually offered a referendum on the proposal and it was the right-wing National Party that delivered the change. After two referenda, the first elections under the new system took place in 1996.

If Labour move to a position of supporting electoral reform, as a number of their MPs have committed to do (12 have signed up to the Good Systems agreement), the New Zealand experience offers a road map for how change might be achieved. It seems unlikely, however, that a Royal Commission would be the appropriate mechanism given that the last commission in the UK reported back in 2000. What other means might therefore exist?

Increasingly, more deliberative democracy options are being considered. France's Convention Citoyenne pour le Climat met for its final session in June 2020. Comprised of 150 randomly selected French citizens, the Convention was tasked to find measures that would support a 40 per cent reduction in greenhouse gases from 1990 levels. With the support of experts and stakeholders, the Convention has developed 149 recommendations over an eight-month period. All of these recommendations have either been referred to a legislature for action or will be put to a public referendum.

A similar approach to determine a fairer voting system could be an option. Deliberative democracy approaches are beginning to be utilised in the UK by some local authorities, for example, the COVID-19 citizens' panel set up by the West Midlands Recovery Co-ordination Group, as well as the climate change assemblies in Oxford and Camden. Arguably, a citizens' assembly or indeed a constitutional convention could negate the need for a referendum by taking a consensual approach to the issue.

Conclusion

A proportional system would be the default if you were setting up a democratic state in the 21st century. The systems set up in the devolved administrations show this. During the COVID-19 pandemic, local systems and accountability have been found wanting as local authorities struggle to cope with budgets reduced during austerity and an overly centralised governance model. At a time when politics seems as divided as it has ever been, and when the government in power is able to act with impunity on issues such as the rule of law and the UK's international standing, it is even more critical that power is in the hands of politicians that are elected fairly by a true consensual majority.

TWO

How could a government actually deliver more housing?

Housing has been such a Cinderella issue for so long that poor policies have been tolerated for decades. Even now, voters are worried about so much else (at the time of writing, coronavirus, jobs and Brexit) that not even 1 per cent of respondents to Ipsos-Mori's long-running poll say that housing is the issue of most concern facing Britain. Moreover, any attempts to deal with the housing problem – both the lack of housing for increasing numbers of households (due to later marriage, divorce and longer lives) and the increasing unaffordability of housing as prices have soared – tend to require long-term solutions that politicians focused on the next election too easily ignore.

Yet, housing probably does more to determine most people's welfare than anything else apart from their income and their health. Homelessness should not scar any rich society. Any prosperous country should surely be able to ensure more living space for its citizens, not less, as in the UK (where new privately built housing for sale now rarely matches the Parker-Morris standards for council housing after the war). Any sensible government should want its people to own and care for their own homes as they want, but not to believe that housing is a get-rich-quick alternative to hard work and building businesses.

One brave option would be to set a clear long-term target either for house-building (as was the case in the 1950s, when Churchill appointed Macmillan as Housing Minister with the warning that it would make or break him) or for house prices. By most estimates, we need between 250,000 and 300,000 new homes a year to meet rising demand and some of the backlog. A clear target would have the effect of focusing attention on government delivery, as well as on the detailed measures needed to improve our record. My own preference would be a target not for the number of homes, but for house prices. (As economists point out, you can set a target for quantity or price but not both.) A house price target could even be highly popular with the younger generation, who rightly want to get on the housing ladder and struggle to pay rent: taking one year with another – over, say, the business cycle – the government could promise that house prices would not fall but would also not rise higher than average earnings (which historically rise by 1–2.5 per cent a year more than prices). This would cap house prices – and rents.

The result would be a government commitment to make housing steadily more affordable: even if house prices rose, they would rise less than earnings so that housing costs would take less of people's income. There would be years when prices rise more and some when they fall. There would also continue to be areas where prices rise sharply and others where they fall. However, overall, the government should take responsibility for ensuring that house prices through the cycle do not fall and do not rise too much.

Stopping an excessive rise is the big problem. So, here are some practical ideas. The first is to start building far more social housing as this would slow down rent rises and make buy-to-let less attractive. (It would also, most fundamentally, improve housing conditions for the poorest.) Any social housing provider (either council or housing association) should be able to borrow money from the exchequer at the same rate as the Treasury's long-term bonds (less than 0.25 per cent for ten-year money) for new-build projects where they can show a positive rate of return from social rent. There is, though, a problem. Farmland can be bought for £8,000 to £12,000 an acre, but as soon as planning permission is granted, that land soars in value to anything from £600,000 to £1 million.[1] If social housing providers could buy at farmland prices, social housing would easily service the debt incurred to build it (and more). However, the calculation is much more marginal if the price includes the award of planning permission, and only makes financial sense for the public sector as a whole after many years once Treasury savings in housing benefit are taken into account. As a result, councils, particularly in urban areas, spend large amounts of time and effort extracting cash, promises to build social housing and community projects from developers under the aegis of section 106, a messy and arbitrary system.[2]

Councils should be able to buy land through an agent, that is, anonymously, and then give themselves planning permission to build without fear that the seller would chase them for any part of the land price rise after planning permission is given. They could even be given back the power to compulsorily purchase land at its existing use value (before planning permission was granted). This would reinstate the situation from 1945 to 1961, when the Land Compensation Act gave the right to owners to be compensated not just for the existing value, but any value in future.[3] This would also allow inner-city councils to assemble reasonable sites, and would give all councils a big incentive to build social housing (and even buy sites to sell on for private development at a profit).

The government also has to work on the private rental market. Local councils have powers to restrict short-term tourist lettings (for example, Airbnb) in areas of housing shortage, and should use them (with a national league table to highlight those who do not). It should also mandate double council tax for any property left vacant for more than three months: at present, there continues to be a worryingly high number of vacant flats in London and other big cities, often bought off-plan by Chinese and other foreign investors who keep them empty because they trust the UK's rule of (property) law more than state-owned banks at home. Checking energy usage is an easy way of identifying empty homes, and councils should have the power to see gas and electricity volumes. The growing trend to build-for-rent should also be encouraged. If necessary, the government could give time-limited tax incentives (lower capital gains tax, or lower corporation tax on profits from rent) to companies that begin build-for-rent within a defined period.

However, the biggest market that needs fixing is owner-occupation, where there have been far too many counterproductive quick fixes (such as subsidies to first-time buyers that merely have the effect of bidding up prices). In the short term, there should be more flexibility about conversion of offices and other commercial premises to housing (particularly in the light of the expected fall in office demand after COVID-19), but there should also be tough building regulations insisting on adequate space and light. Many office buildings are deep, so that a lot of space is far from windows; these are not suitable for conversion. Small builders who have been squeezed out of this market by the high regulatory costs should be encouraged back; there could be automatic 'permitted development' for small sites where the proposal meets building regulations for the area.

There must also be a new towns programme like that of the post-war period (which saw the building of Stevenage, Corby, Milton Keynes, Skelmersdale and so on). With only 6 per cent of the UK's land area built up, and with space and welfare for our housing being steadily squeezed, it is crazy not to identify farmland that can be used for new settlements. How to do it? If reform of the Land Compensation Act 1961 is undertaken, new town corporations could also fund infrastructure from the profits of buying farmland at its existing use value. An alternative proposal (from Tim Leunig) is to ask for offers of land of the necessary size in targeted areas and see what emerges.[4] Not surprisingly, many urban-edge farmers are more interested in farming housing than cattle. The likelihood is that some farmers and estates would be prepared to sell at a small premium to farmland prices rather than wait for the bird in the bush.

The way to make these new towns work well is to improve their infrastructure from the start; here, the obvious model is the Metropolitan Railway (now tube line), which bought land around its stations in the 1930s, building homes and making a tidy profit from rising land values. Crucially, it also introduced fast trains that bypassed several stops so that it could continue to claim that such-and-such a station was within so many minutes of Baker Street. New York City too has express subways that skip five stations at a time. By modifying existing lines – including under- and overpasses through inner-city stops – new towns that are some way from city centres (and outside politically sacrosanct green belts) could be made part of the travel-to-work area and help cap house prices.

The extraordinary gains when farmland wins housing permission show just how crucial land prices are: they are by far and away the largest component of house prices. In the South-East, the cost of the bricks and mortar is typically less than half. However, there is a word of warning here to those tempted by a tax on development land when it is given planning permission: this hobby horse has ridden before in the form of the 1947 development charge, the 1967 betterment levy, the 1973 development gains tax and the 1976 development land tax. All died through asphyxiation by their own complexities.[5] They usually slowed down development because if you tax an activity, you tend to reduce it. Removal of the Land Compensation Act provisions would go a long way but would not be comprehensive since they would only affect councils. There is a better option for the long term that would increase housing supply, capture some of the benefit of public improvements such as new transport infrastructure and improve the quality of our built-up areas.

After all, we all know that the UK has historically underinvested in infrastructure partly because the benefits of what is public investment often flow to private landowners. For example, the cost of London's Jubilee Line was £3.5 billion, of which just £180 million was extracted (with difficulty and some menaces) from the developers of Canary Wharf. However, the value of the property all along the line was estimated to have risen by £13 billion, yet those landowners paid nothing extra towards the line. What if some of that benefit automatically went to the Treasury whenever the public sector funded infrastructure? I rather suspect that the negotiations with the Treasury would be a lot easier, and we might have more infrastructure. A similar windfall for property-owners is operating today around the Elizabeth Line (aka Crossrail), though its latest cost to all of us has escalated to more than £19 billion.

The solution is the land-value tax, a rate calculated on the underlying value of the land rather than the buildings on it. We should tax the land, not the buildings. If nearby infrastructure improves land values, the rateable value goes up. If the council zones an area to allow six-storey buildings, then a two- or three-storey building has the same rateable value as a six-storey building, and the owner has an incentive to improve and expand (or sell to someone who will). The higher building will not attract extra tax. An empty site in a city centre – and there have been some, sometimes disguised as car parks, for decades – would attract the same rate as the building that could be put on it. As a result, developers would have an enormous incentive to build and improve up to the limits set by planners. At present, an empty site costs a developer nothing despite the potential urban blight and effect on neighbours. In future, it should cost something. One result would be the steady and organic renewal of cities.

This land-value tax has been tried elsewhere too, notably, in US cities, the largest of which is Pittsburgh. It has also been implemented in Denmark and Australia. Studies have shown that the long-run result is more construction activity and less wasted space, and less need to expand the footprint of urban settlements. It would also make urban areas work better by helping to fund public infrastructure.

Look at the Elizabeth Line again: a study by property consultancy GVA predicts an increase in the value of nearby land of £20.1 billion.[6] The extra rental value would, in time, be at least 4 per cent of that total, or some £800 million a year. Less than a tenth of that annual gain would have been enough to fund the interest on bonds to finance the whole of the construction, including overruns. Moreover, a tax of 10 per cent of the increase in land value would still leave 90 per cent of the gains in the hands of private landowners. No other proposed tax would be either as fair or as effective in funding public transport investment and raising revenue for local authorities to fund other improvements. As a result, it has even been backed by some far-sighted landlords who understand the failings of the market. These estimates of property value and rents do, though, highlight the importance of moving gradually and slowly. Commercial rents are only renegotiated infrequently, and any extra tax must be levied after rents have increased and they are payable out of the landlord's extra cash flow.

A land-value tax would also tackle a large market failure in many depressed urban areas. In the South-East, there is a paradox of soaring house prices at the same time as a substantial amount of land is unused and underused. Some estimates have suggested that more than 350,000 houses could be built on previously developed (brownfield) land in London. What accounts for this mystery?

If we are to believe the Barker Review in 2004 – the last intensive look at the problem – it is all a question of the planning system. Certainly, that is part of the answer. Planning should be simpler and more rules-based, so that it is less subjective and more predictable. However, what is also important is that the market does not provide adequate incentives for landowners and developers to redevelop where they should – in existing urban areas – rather than sucking in ever-greater swathes of greenfield land. At present, many owners of urban land allow it to fall into disuse or underuse because there is an extra cost to redeveloping brownfield sites (in preparing and sometimes decontaminating them) and no cost in failing to develop. The significance of a land-value tax is that landowners would have an incentive to immediately develop sites that fall into disuse, or to sell to someone who could. Paying an annual charge for land, regardless of what is built on it, concentrates minds wonderfully.

In the US cities that tax buildings less heavily than land, the effect has been dramatic. As John Norquist, President of the

Congress for the New Urbanism and the acclaimed former Democrat Mayor of Milwaukee, said: 'It's been great for Pittsburgh. You almost can't find an empty lot in downtown Pittsburgh. They've done a lot of things wrong in Pittsburgh, but one thing they did right was having this land value taxation so there's no incentive to have an empty lot.'[7]

A tax on land values would need to be introduced slowly, perhaps starting (as the Liberal Democrats have proposed) with the reform of business rates. However, the evidence is that it would help to fix our failing land markets. It would make a crucial contribution to the financing of social improvements. It could shift private incentives so that areas do not fall into unfashionable disuse because of blight. It would provide an incentive for developers to bring forward plans that are tailored to social needs. Where such taxes are applied, there are higher levels of construction activity and a better-looking urban environment – and more housing ... which is what we need.

Conclusion

Governments need a clear target – either for home-building or house prices – to hold them to the task of increasing building. There are many potential measures. There should be more social housing by allowing local government and housing associations to borrow money at the Treasury interest rate, and by allowing councils to buy land anonymously – at current use value – prior to granting themselves planning permission. We should even consider restoring the council's right to compulsorily purchase at current use values, a right that enabled the post-war boom in social house-building. Empty properties should be discouraged with increased council tax in areas of housing stress. We need more new towns with fast rail connections to urban areas, and also new town corporations empowered to buy farmland at current use value. There are all short-term fixes; the long-run health of the land and housing market would be assured by a land-value tax, taxing the land but not the buildings on it, and thereby encouraging maximum development within the planning guidelines. A land-value tax would also fund infrastructure improvements (like the Jubilee Line or Crossrail) from a small part of rising rents around the development. Housing needs to be reinstated by radical governments as one of the key goals of progressive policy.

Notes

[1] At the time of the Kate Barker Review of housing policy in 2004, the review cited an increase in the value of a hectare of land from £7,534 to £1.23 million following planning permission.

[2] Section 106 of the Town and Country Planning Act 1990.

[3] Daniel Bentley (2017) *The Land Question: Fixing the Dysfunction at the Root of the Housing Crisis*, London: Civitas.

[4] Tim Leunig outlines community land auctions, a scheme nearly taken up by the Coalition but ultimately blocked by the Conservatives. See Tim Leunig (2011) *In My Back Yard*, London: CentreForum.

[5] See Christopher Huhne (2004) 'Land campaign – why we should follow Pittsburgh', *New Statesman*, September.

[6] The first study commissioned by Crossrail dramatically underestimated the impact, and the second study cited here

may ultimately also fall short. See GVA (2017) *Crossrail Property Impact and Regeneration Study 2012–2026*, London: GVA.

[7] Mayor John Norquist of Milwaukee, Wisconsin, 26 January 1999, https://www.cooperative-individualism.org/land-question_m-q.htm

THREE

How will technology change the future of work?

Ian Kearns

Unhelpful beginnings

For politicians not paying much attention, there is an easy, plausible line to take when pushed to say something about technology and the future of work. That line goes something like this: automation is going to replace lots of jobs in the coming years, and to deal with it, we need to upskill people to do the jobs that technology will not be able to do. As a narrative, it is plausible because it is not entirely wrong. However, if social democrats and liberals want to be future-ready, they are going to have to come up with a far more rounded and comprehensive answer to what amounts to a historic process of economic transformation.

A lively debate is under way on how technology adoption is going to impact the labour market of the future. Some argue that technology change is going to create massive unemployment; others that automation anxiety is nothing new and that previous waves of technology adoption have created at least as many jobs as they have replaced.

Neither extreme is that helpful. The first position tends to downplay the extent to which new jobs may be created and to assume that the pace of change will be far quicker than is likely to be the case. It sees automation almost as an event, not as a longer-term historical process.

The second position is far too sanguine in its assumption that just because previous periods of technology adoption have ultimately created as many jobs as they replaced, this will inevitably be the outcome this time. It is also blind to the social devastation that may accompany the transition to the age of automation.

As Daniel Susskind pointed out in his book *A World Without Work*, during the Industrial Revolution:

> the unemployment rate in Britain remained relatively low. But at the same time whole industries were decimated, with lucrative crafts like hand weaving and candle making turned into profitless pastimes. Communities were hollowed out and entire cities thrust into decline. It is noteworthy that real wages in Britain barely rose – a measly 4 per cent rise in total from 1760 to 1820. Meanwhile food became more expensive, diets were poorer, infant mortality worsened, and life expectancy fell. People were quite literally diminished … average

physical heights fell to their lowest ever levels on account of this hardship.[1]

What we know

What we do know is that technology in the form of robotics, automation and remote working is already having a major impact on the labour market, and has been for some time. This change is manifest not only in sectors like manufacturing, but also in financial services and insurance, where fin-tech and insure-tech are automating tasks previously carried out by people.

Second, we know that the rate and impact of technology adoption is also being accelerated by the COVID-19 pandemic. Social distancing requirements and instructions to stay at home impacted the availability of some labour at the onset of the pandemic. This has had what economists have called 'automation-forcing' effects. These can be seen in cases such as increased reliance on security cameras rather than on security guards, increased use of robots to clean workplaces and keep warehouses functioning, and in greater automation of meat-packing facilities. The massively increased reliance on telepresence for remote working has also changed the geography of economic activity, quite possibly permanently.

Third, we also know that we live in an age where machines and automated systems are becoming more and more capable of taking on tasks previously performed by people. The uncertainty is not about whether this is happening, but about the speed at which it will continue to happen, and what its wider economic and social consequences will be.

Workers are not only noticing, but anxious. One survey of UK employees found that 50 per cent of them thought their jobs would be replaced by technology within the next 20 years. Many are profoundly worried, even scared, about what this might mean not only for themselves, but also for the prospects of their children. If they want to be taken seriously, social democrats and liberals need to demonstrate to voters that they understand the future that is emerging, that they are thinking deeply about how to handle it and that they have answers.

Better education and training

Responding to the situation through changed and improved education and training is important, especially in the short term. It can help prepare people to do the tasks that machines either cannot do or will not do very well for the foreseeable future.

It is also possible, and obviously a good idea, to invest in developing the skills needed to build and code the systems, robots and other machines that will be doing a lot of the work that used to be done by people. Such ideas can smooth the transition, and can buy policymakers and societies time.

We are not currently doing enough. Our education system is still teaching people to do all sorts of things machines are already good at; it is failing to focus more imaginatively on the development of aptitudes that machines are less good at; and both the quality of teaching in computer science and the number of pupils and students gaining a good grounding in it are nowhere near the level needed for this to amount to a convincing national strategy. Most countries, including our own, are also still failing to adapt and take advantage of the ways in which technology can deliver education to far larger numbers of students in a personalised, more flexible and more cost-effective way.

Even if we were getting these issues right, however, and pushing on from there to make lifelong learning opportunities more of a reality, there would still be profound limitations with this approach. Telling people to retrain from the jobs that are being replaced to the ones that are newly coming on stream is easier said than done. If retraining is expensive, some people will not be able to afford it, and for older workers in particular, they may not have enough of their working lives ahead of them to recoup the investment. Some will find it hard to develop new skills. Also, some of the work available will be in the wrong place geographically or not a good fit for the identity and value systems of those needing a job. Of course, none of this comes close to being a sufficient response if there is, over time, simply not enough work to go around anyway.

This may well be where we are headed. As Max Tegmark points out in his brilliant exploration of artificial intelligence (AI), *Life 3.0*, machines are already moving way beyond routine tasks and becoming good at activities that require creativity and empathy. They are even reaching the point at which they can start to build themselves.

More and better education and training, then, can buy us time in which to find other solutions but other solutions are likely to be needed. A more rounded approach to the implications of technology change and automation would consider the issues of taxation, income distribution, capital ownership and labour rights, at a minimum.

Fairer taxation

If more work is done in future by machines and less by people, tax receipts from income earned in return for labour will shrink. A central, inescapable, question will be how to fill this funding gap.

The practical options seem clear. Those people still in work, whose skills are in high demand in the age of increased automation and who can therefore command high salaries, will need to be taxed more. This would not be enough on its own, of course, so taxes on capital and wealth will need to be revisited too.

Finding a way to tax the largest and wealthiest companies more will be particularly important. The current jurisdiction hopping and tax avoidance practised by these companies is a moral affront. Some of the big technology players, backed by armies of accountants who seem to think it professionally and socially respectable to facilitate tax avoidance, are paying tax rates lower than the poorest people in society.

Finding a politically viable way to rebalance the tax system, while making sure the changes introduced do not choke off needed and welcome aspects of innovation, will be one of the central tasks faced by progressive politicians the world over as the age of automation gathers pace.

New approaches to income distribution

Another huge question concerns the mechanism by which incomes will be distributed. If income generated in return for labour is less and less the mechanism through which distribution occurs, then what mechanism will replace the distributive function of the labour market? The welfare system can help, but in relation to employment, it is designed to support people who are temporarily out of work while they get back into work. If they cannot get back into work, then we are dealing with a more permanent problem, and as the scale and pace of automation increases, that problem may well become a social crisis.

This is where the idea of something like a citizens' or universal basic income comes in. The idea has been floating around for more than 200 years and, in more recent times, has been seen by some as a necessity in the context of the COVID-19 pandemic. The fact that governments around the world, including our own, have stepped in with direct payments to citizens to help them get through the crisis is often viewed as a historic, Rubicon-crossing moment.

The backdrop of increased automation may, however, be an even more persuasive reason as to why something like this will need to be explored. Those who simply dismiss it as too expensive can only plausibly do so by arguing that automation is not leading and will not lead to less work for people, on the one hand, or that they have a better solution to the income distribution problem in a world of less work, on the other. To this author, it seems they are far from winning the argument on the first proposition and have not even started thinking about the second.

None of this is to say that the politics of something like a universal basic income is easy. There are disagreements over the appropriate level of any payments, and over just how 'universal' it should be. There are also big questions over its proponents' ability to persuade the public of the merits of such a scheme in the short term.

One of the biggest challenges of a universal basic income politically, however, is likely to be to find a way of implementing it that binds people together rather than driving them apart. If there is less work available, more people will be reliant on those who are in work. The potential for feelings of resentment from those who are in work and shame among those who are not will be large. These sentiments already exist in the welfare debate and they surface even when the payments being made are smaller than they would be under a universal basic income. Social democrats and liberals campaigning for a universal basic income cannot just wish this political problem away.

Wider capital ownership

Managing this problem almost certainly requires nesting the idea of a universal basic income in a wider set of changes needed to address inequality. A world of increased automation, if left to unfold according to its dynamics and devices, will be a world where capital is increasingly owned by a few while the majority live precarious lives on the edge of poverty. If nothing is done to diversify and equalise asset ownership, the politics of income distribution is likely to be toxic and plagued by those sentiments of resentment and shame.

Here, there are real options that need to be explored and grasped. The creation of sovereign wealth funds owned by citizens, where the fund invests in a diverse portfolio of assets and can pay dividends directly to citizens, could not only contribute to the costs of something like a universal basic income, but also transform its politics. The payments could not be badged by opponents as flowing from a 'magic money tree' or as rewards for indolence as they would instead be entitlements flowing from a stake in publicly owned assets.

Other ideas being pushed by Andrew Yang, the former candidate for the Democratic nomination for president in the US, are also worth exploring in this regard. Yang has set up a Citizen Data Dividend project in California, in which citizens are being encouraged to come together to negotiate a price for the data they are handing over to big tech, and out of which big tech is making large (and frequently untaxed) profits. Again, the idea is to establish asset ownership (in this case, personal data being the asset) and to leverage revenue from it on behalf of citizens.

Strengthening the power of labour

Responses to technology transformation through new policies on taxation, income distribution and capital ownership are likely to be gradual, both in their introduction and effect. In the more immediate future, there will also be a need to use public power more effectively to protect workers from the maelstrom of change.

At a minimum, social democrats and liberals should argue for the law to be used to increase the rights of those in insecure, part-time and precarious work. Public sector workers doing essential work of high social value for insufficient reward should receive pay rises. Trade unions should be encouraged and helped to grow their memberships, and the more they can use digital channels and platforms to aid both better worker organisation and greater union penetration among the young, the better. A world of increased automation is a world in need of J.K. Galbraith's countervailing power of labour.

Technology has the potential to make lives better, reduce the burden of work and contribute solutions to some of humanity's biggest problems. However, if we do not grapple with the problems and challenges touched on in this chapter, it could just as easily lead to economic division, social crisis and political strife.

Conclusion

Change is coming and we can use education to increase skill levels within the workforce to mitigate the impact; however, a more fundamental correction is required. Using education and training will help people who lose their jobs due to technological change. However, we also need to find ways to ensure that income inequality does not grow. We can do this through new approaches to income redistribution, wider capital ownership, possibly a universal basic income and empowering marginalised workers by increasing the power of organised labour.

Note

[1] Daniel Susskind (2020) *A World Without Work*, London: Allen Lane, Penguin Random House, p 18.

FOUR

Can better public ownership promote efficiency and social justice?

Roger Liddle

At the December 2019 general election, Labour stood on a manifesto of extensive renationalisation and state intervention in the economy. There had been nothing like it since 1983, when Gerald Kaufman memorably described the party's manifesto as 'the longest suicide note in history'. The Corbyn leadership had successfully brought back public ownership as a central plank in Labour's platform.

In so doing, they reopened one of the most divisive ideological questions in Labour history. The old Clause IV part 4 of Labour's 1918 Constitution defined the aims and objects of the party as the 'common ownership of the means of production, distribution and exchange'. In practice, this commitment proved to be far more rhetorical and symbolic than a statement of how the party saw its central mission. Yet, it remained emblazoned on the party's membership card.

Its critics, both inside and outside the party, had for decades objected that this relic of 1918 completely misrepresented how a social democratic party should see its relationship with the private sector and the market economy. Tony Blair's 1995 reform of Clause IV was a crucial act of social democratic revisionism, at long last liberating the party, in the language of the time, to come to terms with modernity. A quarter of a century later, the Corbyn leadership were determined to turn the clock back.

In the very particular political context of the 2019 general election, Labour's renewed commitment to public ownership passed by with relatively little notice. Yet, for most of the party's history, this had been the crucial ideological battleground between, on the one hand, Labour pragmatists, revisionists and modernisers and, on the other, self-styled socialist transformationists. This chapter will first remind readers of the history of this long struggle. It will put the British debate in the context of the ideological development of European social democracy. It will then review the respective record of nationalisation and privatisation in Britain's post-Second World War history and discuss what might have changed in recent times to call for a rethink of the lessons of the past. Finally, it will consider what we presently know of where Keir Starmer stands on these issues. It concludes that while old-style public ownership might occasionally be inevitable as a last resort, an extension of new forms of public equity should find a useful, but modest and non-ideological, place in a modern industrial policy designed to promote decent, well-paid jobs for the future and tackle the gross regional inequalities that scar our country.

The Labour debate on public ownership, nationalisation and state control

Early socialist support for public ownership had its origins in the view that the root of all evil in society was the pursuit of private profit. In the social conditions of late 19th-century Britain, it is easy to see how this idea appealed to progressive idealists and socialists of many different stripes. Britain had pioneered the Industrial Revolution and made itself the richest country in the world – but at an appalling cost in social misery and stark inequality.

Christian socialists and humanists advanced an ethical critique of private profit. It owed much more to the Book of Revelation than *Das Kapital*. The New Jerusalem they sought to build could not be based on greed. Greed poisoned human relations. They wanted to build a society with a new ethic of personal relationships based on love, compassion and mutual respect. In this ideal society, there could be no basis for the economic exploitation of one human being by another.

In time, ethical socialists came to realise that their principal goal was not the abolition of profit per se, but the achievement of greater social equality, in a more broadly defined sense than simply economics. Keir Hardie got there first. For him, equality for women and opposition to colonialism and racial discrimination were of equal importance with economic issues. He campaigned tirelessly for the right to work and the living wage; in themselves, notable reforms of capitalism but not seeking to abolish private enterprise.[1] Together with 'Home Rule All Round', this placed him, as a Scot representing a Welsh constituency, more in the Gladstonian and Radical Liberal tradition than the Marxist one. For good measure, Keir Hardie was also a strong advocate of proportional representation!

Where, then, did Clause IV originate from? One could point to the syndicalist ideas that led to demands for workers' control and G.D.H. Cole's advocacy of guild socialism. However, these ephemeral ideas never got far among the trade unions, who prioritised protecting and extending workers' rights through collective bargaining. Equally important may have been ideas popular among Radical Liberals of the Edwardian era, such as returning the ownership of land to the people. Also, the municipal achievements of 'gas and water' socialism supported the belief that public ownership could be more efficient than private. Furthermore, as social and economic conditions began to deteriorate badly in the coal mines, especially after the First World War, the notion that the only solution lay in public ownership attracted influential support well beyond the workers in the industry itself.

Then there was the lingering influence of Marxist ideas and the immediate excitement of the Russian Revolution. For the early socialists attracted to Marxism, profits were the engine of capitalist exploitation and economic inequality: if profits could be seized by the workers through winning political power, either through democracy or revolution, an equal society became possible. Although the Russian Revolution of 1917 created some temporary enthusiasm in Britain, for example, among some of the leaders of 'Red Clydeside', it had little lasting appeal on the British Left: from the early 1920s, Labour conferences consistently excluded communists from Labour membership by overwhelming majorities. Ramsay Macdonald's great achievement, well before his infamous 1931 betrayal, was in committing Labour to the 'parliamentary road' in which society would 'evolve' towards socialism through a process of gradualist democratic reform. In this, Macdonald was greatly influenced by the great revisionist German social democrat Edouard Bernstein, who had become a friend before the First World War.

Some prominent Fabians were, however, impressed by aspects of the Soviet system, especially the commitment to central planning. In the process, they turned a shameful blind eye to the horrendous human rights abuses of Leninist and Stalinist Russia. The lesson they drew from the Bolshevik experiment, which suited the Fabian temperament, was the idea that planning was more efficient than the capitalist free market; it left a long-lasting imprint on the mindset of the British Left.

After much internal party turbulence in the 1930s, a new Labour generation (including Hugh Dalton, Hugh Gaitskell, Douglas Jay and Evan Durbin) began to recognise that their democratic socialist mission would be to reform capitalism, not replace it. Keynesianism offered the compelling prospect of economic tools to stabilise the economy and abolish the curse of mass unemployment. Ernie Bevin, as Andrew Adonis describes in his brilliant new biography, was one of Labour's earliest converts. The wartime Beveridge Report established a popular consensus behind the idea of a comprehensive welfare state, funded by a mix of general taxation and compulsory NICs. This, it should be noted, was a scheme for the 'many', paid for by the 'many' – alongside redistributive taxation, of course – in sharp contrast to Labour's 2019 ludicrous claim that all additional social spending would be paid for by taxes on the richest 5 per cent of the population.

The war was also seen to vindicate the idea of planning. Victory had been achieved by mobilising the whole resources of the country through an all-encompassing system of economic controls and rationing. Labour's association with these ideas proved a mixed blessing for the party in the post-war years as the electorate tired of rationing and shared sacrifice. The Conservatives rebuilt their political position by appealing directly to a newly prosperous generation of housewives and consumers.

Labour, though, had developed a coherent policy for selective acts of nationalisation as an essential pillar of a 'planned' economy. The argument was made primarily on grounds of 'efficiency', not workers' control or the appropriation by the people of capitalist profit. The model was Herbert Morrison's pioneering establishment of the London Transport Board in the 1929–31 Labour government, which became the basis for the Attlee government's post-war nationalisation programme. The nationalisation of coal, the railways, gas, electricity and iron and steel were all argued for on efficiency grounds as they were sectors where the private sector was failing the nation.

In that era, Aneurin Bevan was right to describe these sectors as the 'commanding heights' of the economy but, by implication, he wanted to go much further. In the last years of the Attlee government, Morrison successfully blocked this ambition with a policy of 'consolidation'; in practice, this meant building on Labour's existing achievements in expanding the state sector, with only limited further extensions of public ownership to be argued case by case. Not only was this designed to rebut Tory propaganda that Labour wanted to nationalise every garage and corner shop; it was also intended to reassure business corporations that they should see Labour as their partner, not a sworn enemy. In practice, Labour supported a 'mixed economy' in which private companies continued to make profits in accordance with how innovative and competitive they were. The Attlee government deliberately left untouched the large corporations that dominated manufacturing. When Labour did venture there, as in its proposal in 1951 to nationalise the sugar monopoly, this led Tate and Lyle to finance a highly effective anti-socialist campaign.

Labour began to develop other solutions for the problem of monopolists acting against the public interest. Where profits were excessive, the Attlee government for the first time put in place new public institutions with a remit to control (and, in the last analysis, break up) monopolies and curb restrictive practices.

The Bevanites fiercely opposed these policy developments, arguing that further nationalisation was the essence of socialist advance. The serious intellectual challenge to the Left's position came in 1956 with the publication of Crosland's *Future of Socialism*,[2] the best book of social democratic theory ever produced in English, and written in a sparkling style. The intellectual depth and precise logic of Crosland's arguments are impossible to summarise. He defined the central social democratic goal as greater equality and demonstrated that further public ownership had little, if anything, to contribute to progress towards it. Crosland's ideas were deliberately provocative. Michael Foot famously denounced them as nothing other than a gross betrayal of socialism.

The 1950s witnessed a fierce battle between revisionists and fundamentalists. This culminated in Hugh Gaitskell's failed

1960 attempt to remove Clause IV from the party constitution. However in the decade after Labour's defeat in 1951, the tone of Labour's position changed from pledges of further nationalisation of whole industries to clear support for a mixed economy, with an increased emphasis on alternative forms of competitive public enterprise, though all coupled within a continued rhetorical commitment to unspecific notions of 'planning'. Extraordinary as it may now seem, in the early 1960s, mainstream Labour figures on what we would now call the 'soft Left', like Richard Crossman, were still arguing that Soviet planning would prove more efficient than Western capitalism. However, he was not alone: this fear was shared by public policymakers on both sides of the Atlantic!

Harold Wilson managed to briefly quell Labour's ideological conflicts with his famous 1963 conference speech that married science to socialism, which he described in terms of 'purposive planning'. Labour would devise a 'national plan'. What Wilson precisely had in mind remained obscure, but the intellectual backdrop to his electoral success as the champion of modernity was the public's growing realisation that UK growth was falling badly behind that of the Common Market Six: 'indicative planning' seemed to work well in France and, to an extent, Italy. For Wilson, planning involved a whole panoply of reforms led by an active state: modernisation of the state itself and its civil service; increased public investment in science and the industries of the future; investment incentives for business growth in the regions; a huge expansion in universities and industrial training; and the spread of comprehensive education. Public intervention was also argued for to reorganise failing sectors of the economy, in partnership with the private sector, through a new state body, the Industrial Reorganisation Corporation. The only industry taken into classic public ownership in the 1964–70 government was iron and steel, which the Churchill government had de-nationalised.

Unfortunately, Wilson's ambition to achieve 4 per cent per annum growth was never fulfilled and the 1967 devaluation was seen as a significant defeat. Yet, in the perspective of history, the 1960s were the period when Britain enjoyed the fastest rate of economic growth since 1945, the biggest ever expansion of the welfare state and an era of the most radical social reform. However, the Labour Left bought into the Conservative argument that this had been a period of socialist failure. An invigorated Left was bolstered by a new generation of trade union leaders sympathetic to growing shop-floor militancy and opposed to the wage restraint that Labour's 'planned' incomes policies had demanded, always an aspect of their general calls for socialist planning that made the Labour Left look inconsistent in their attachment to 'free collective bargaining'. The role of planning and public ownership in the economy became the battleground of further intense dispute between social democrats and left-wingers from the 1970s to the late 1980s.

Under the leadership of Tony Benn, the Left became hooked on the concept of 'an alternative industrial strategy'. Compulsory 'planning agreements' would force private business to sign legally binding contracts that required boards to follow the dictates of ministers; indeed, political appointees would be put in the driving seat on most big company boards. To bolster and extend this 'democratic' control of industry, the public sector would take significant equity stakes in top companies across the whole economy – a proposal that Harold Wilson, now leader of the opposition, point blank refused to accept at the 1973 conference.

The 1974–79 Labour governments became a war of attrition between ministers and Labour's National Executive, which came increasingly under the control of the Labour Left. Public ownership grew rapidly but mainly of industries such as shipbuilding and British Leyland that were on the point of bankruptcy and proved to be costly 'lame ducks'. After Labour's defeat in 1979, the conflict intensified between an emboldened Left and a besieged parliamentary Labour Party, many of whom were condemned as traitors. The battle over 'Bennery' provided the context for both the 1981 SDP split and Jeremy Corbyn's political apprenticeship. It continued fiercely in the Labour Party after Labour lost office in 1979 and through most of the period where Thatcherism was taking the country in the opposite direction with the assault on trade union power, privatisation and the reassertion of the values of the free market. While the world around him changed profoundly, Corbyn's consistent faith in Bennery never faltered. Consistency is normally seen as a political virtue but is it better to be consistent and wrong, or inconsistent and accept the realities of a changing world?

European social democratic revisionism

As Labour failed to heal its ideological divisions, fellow social democrats on the Continent followed a different path. The Swedish Social Democrats, arguably the world's most successful centre-left party, had never made public ownership part of their programme; rather, they struck a bargain of their own with Swedish capitalism. In return for the Social Democrats' continued acceptance of private ownership, private business accepted higher taxes to pay for a welfare state and stronger trade unions with entrenched collective bargaining rights to defend employee interests.

The German SPD had its roots in Marxism. Divided by Bernstein's revisionism, it never fully came to terms with it. Yet, from the 1930s to the 1950s, it stayed true to the 'Democracy' enshrined in the party's name with its heroic resistance to Nazism and then, after the Second World War, its refusal to be subsumed by communism. Yet, at the Bad Godesburg conference in 1960, the SPD, encouraged by a new generation of leaders of the quality of Willy Brandt, famously abandoned its quasi-Marxist commitment to public ownership and economic planning. Its slogan from that era – 'the market wherever possible, planning wherever necessary' – would not be a bad starting point for the post-Corbyn Labour Party.

The only major Continental socialist party to have seriously embraced an extension of nationalisation and state control were the French socialists. In the Fourth Republic, after the withdrawal of the communists from a tense post-war coalition, the Section Francaise de Internationale ouvriere (SFIO) generally allied with the republican and Catholic forces of the centre, against the communists and Gaullists, to build a French version of a social market economy anchored in a new vision for European integration. De Gaulle's seizure of power in 1958 marginalised the Left in French politics for the best part of two decades. It ended only when Francois Mitterrand won the presidency in 1981 on a common platform with the communists. This included plans for extensive nationalisation and state intervention. Politically, Mitterrand's strategy proved to be of some genius: the communists entered the government but were then marginalised, and their electoral base eroded and ultimately collapsed. Mitterrand won two terms and was president for 14 years. However, the socialist programme, on which he had been elected, lasted little more than two years and ended in a grave financial crisis. Mitterrand and his Finance Minister, Jacques Delors, chose the stability of the franc over sticking with France's failed turn to the Left. From then on, they focused all their principal energies – Mitterrand as President of France and Delors as President of the European Commission – on strengthening European integration, which became their huge joint legacy in history.

The collapse of the Soviet Union in 1990 finally put paid to the idea that Soviet notions of centrally planned efficiency would deliver better living standards and life opportunities for working people than the social market economy of Western Europe. When the socialists returned to power in France in 1997, under Lionel Jospin as Prime Minister, cohabiting with the centre-right President Jacques Chirac, they refused to reverse the privatisation of the industries Mitterrand had nationalised 15 years earlier; indeed, they went on to complete the centre-right's privatisation programme. Jospin, himself a notable intellect, famously proclaimed his belief in a 'market economy, but not a market society.'[3]

By the 1990s, the notion that socialism meant state control had become politically toxic. It was striking that none of the new democracies that emerged from the collapse of the Soviet Union voted in free elections to maintain state socialism.

Instead, they opted to suffer the terrible pain of transition to a market economy. More modern examples of state-run economies by less democratic methods, such as North Korea and Venezuela, have done nothing to contradict this conclusion of history. There have, of course, been examples of the 'developmental state', notably, the Asian Tigers and the People's Republic of China, from which we should try to learn. However, these countries are very different in culture to Europe, even where democracy has developed strong roots, which is certainly not the case with China.

Nationalisation and privatisation in Britain

While the record of nationalisation in post-war Britain was, at best, mixed, it had some successes. Nationalisation of the coal mines replaced a generation of private owners who had failed to invest in the industry and, in the interwar years, pursued an appalling policy of cutting wages and extending miners' hours to keep pits open and protect their profitability. Electricity nationalisation led to the extension of supply to all corners of the UK as a public service obligation (in stark contrast to the patchy coverage today of the private sector suppliers of broadband). The creation of a national grid facilitated the construction of a new generation of huge, much more efficient, power stations, both coal and nuclear, to meet the nation's power needs. The gas industry's achievement in converting supply from localised dirty coal gas to clean natural gas was a technological triumph.

Initially, nationalisation transformed labour relations. In the Attlee cabinet, Bevin and Morrison had a massive row about how the nationalised industries should be run. Bevin wanted to appoint serving trade union officials to their boards. Morrison was fiercely opposed – and won the argument. Instead, former trade unionists were appointed to the new boards, often as personnel directors. In the case of the electricity industry, the former Trades Union Congress (TUC) General Secretary, Walter Citrine, became its first chair, establishing models of good labour relations that succeeded for decades. However, the breakdown of the post-war industrial relations consensus from the 1960s onwards, and the emergence of a new generation of militant trade union leaders, of which Arthur Scargill was the most notorious example, did much to discredit nationalisation. Frequent strikes, and threats of strikes, created the political conditions for the public acceptability of privatisation.

Also, ministers could not resist the temptation to interfere directly in public industries. For some, this was the whole point of nationalisation – political control. However, it had serious consequences for good, efficient management. Price freezes were periodically imposed, pushing industries into deficit and depriving them of the surpluses for necessary investment. In practice, this strengthened the iron grip of the Treasury over key management decisions. Bad mistakes were made in backing major investment programmes for industrial policy purposes, most notoriously, the Advanced Gas-cooled Reactor (AGR) programme of nuclear power stations, of which the leadership of the Central Electricity Generating Board were passionate advocates.

By the 1980s, voters had tired of the nationalised industries. The political debate about their future resembled 'constant frontier wars', as Roy Jenkins memorably described them: Conservatives determined to cut the public sector down to size; and Labour to reverse any interference with the sacred cow of public ownership. Without a political consensus behind it, nationalisation had no long-term future. Instead, Margaret Thatcher made privatisation the received wisdom, introducing a model of privatisation combined with regulation, independent of both government and the privatised industry, which was exported to dozens of countries in the world. It looked good at the time.

Margaret Thatcher owed the domestic acceptability of privatisation, in part, to the Conservative decision to press ahead with council house sales, an electorally brilliant stroke that appealed to aspirational working-class voters. (Labour opposed a measure that, not for the first time, a clear majority of Labour voters supported.) This was followed up by the share giveaways of the early privatisations; in the mid-1980s, media commentators were full of excitement at the prospect of a new people's capitalism. While this eventually turned to nought as the new shareholders, in the main, quickly cashed in on their ill-gotten capital gains at taxpayer expense, public ownership and nationalisation looked like ideas whose time had passed.

Frankly, privatisation did overcome some of nationalisation's problems. Privatised boards were free of detailed ministerial oversight. Managers were set free to manage. Investment could be planned over a longer term and was arguably more efficient. Regulators controlled maximum prices and bore down on costs, meaning that the industries became much leaner and fitter, with fewer staff exercising clearer responsibilities. Competition was introduced in some sectors, though the incumbent companies often tried their best to resist or weaken its effectiveness. In part, this was the fault of the way the industries had been privatised in order to maximise the financial return to the Treasury. However, in part, some parts of the privatised sector are 'natural monopolies'. How can one have effective competition in water supply or, for that matter, the cables that for the last lap of connection supply broadband to the home?

Regulators proved to have limited powers and, in some cases, an apparent reluctance to use them. For example, top pay soared across the whole private sector in the 1990s and 2000s as part of a new business self-confidence that the Thatcher revolution was here to stay. This was not the result of privatisation per se, though its apparent success fostered a culture that there was nothing to be ashamed of in high rewards.

The US experience of the regulation of privately owned utilities was full of warnings of the danger of 'regulatory capture', which generated a whole genre of political science and economics literature. The regulators proved incapable of tackling financial engineering that encouraged the utility sector to load up their balance sheets with debt. High gearing greatly inflated profits and dividends in the immediate term, in effect, by taking profits from the future to pay the business' present owners. If those owners were private equity, they would then sell the company on, having extracted their pound of flesh. Privatised companies then became more expert at organising their affairs (quite legally) to minimise their corporate tax burden.

When Labour won power in 1997, Gordon Brown imposed a huge £5 billion windfall tax on privatised industry profits. Part of the tax revenues financed a jobs programme for the young unemployed. However, by its nature, the windfall tax was an unrepeatable 'one-off'. Labour missed an opportunity to strengthen the powers of industry regulators, which should have involved powers to intervene in the financial strategies dreamt up by their merchant banks and private equity owners. This remains the policy tool to which progressives should first look.

The renationalisation plans of Labour's 2019 manifesto were flawed in key ways:

- There was deliberately no clarity on how Labour would compensate shareholders for the enforced purchase of their shareholdings by the government. John McDonnell said this would be a matter for Parliament, without committing Labour to full shareholder compensation. Any attempt to enforce the public purchase of shares at below a fair assessment of their market value would lead to justifiable charges of unfair expropriation. Nor would it have hit the 'capitalists', who, in many cases, would already have walked away with the pickings of their financial engineering. Pension funds, who are major shareholders of utility stocks (because of their dependable dividend flows), would be legally obligated by their fiduciary duties to their members to take legal action against the UK government. If Labour went down the McDonnell route, innumerable legal challenges and huge delays would have resulted.
- Vocal disputes about shareholder valuation would damage the British government's creditworthiness on the international markets. This would prove a dangerous path to follow given the continuing need to finance at low interest

rates a massive public debt that now exceeds £1 trillion. A loss of international confidence could push up the costs of servicing the public debt, with disastrous consequences for the state's ability to fund public services.

- Labour argued that by getting rid of 'excessive profits', prices could be reduced at the same time as the surpluses generated by the newly nationalised industries would pay the costs of servicing the debt that had been issued to compulsorily buy the shares. This would only be true if less than full compensation was to be paid. Moreover, who was to decide what would be the right level of prices to set? If ministers, then all the old objections to unpredictable ministerial interference come into play. Nor is it clear, for example, that if Labour is serious about radically eliminating carbon emissions and implementing the Green New Deal, energy prices should come down. Similarly, with water supply, higher prices may be needed to meet the industry's environmental obligations. These are clear cases where populism and principle are in conflict.

- Labour promised that new public companies would not be run like the old nationalised industry boards; instead, their boards would include representatives of workers and consumers. But how would these representatives be chosen and to whom would they be accountable and for what objectives? If the worker representatives were trade union officials, how could they sit on 'both sides of the table' when pay and conditions came to be negotiated? And by what institutional means would a welcome 'consumer voice' be channelled?

- Trade union supporters of renationalisation saw this as a route to the restoration of national-level collective bargaining in publicly owned industries. The taxpayer would once again be at risk as the funder of last resort. Trade unionists may rile at this question – but Labour should be in no doubt that this how the Conservatives would react to every disputed public sector wage claim. Furthermore, the privatised industries are not sectors of the economy characterised by low pay and insecurity, where public policies to strengthen the position of trade unions are entirely justified.

The public ownership commitments of the 2019 manifesto firmly moved Labour outside the European social democratic mainstream. Many European social democrats were initially attracted to Corbyn because they shared with him a strong commitment against austerity and rising inequality. However, while European social democratic parties have been the strongest supporters of a European Recovery Plan (some would have liked to have seen even more ambition in the plan that the European Council eventually agreed this July), no mainstream social democratic party has brought back public ownership as a central part of its policy programme.

The challenge facing Keir Starmer

Keir Starmer's election as Labour leader in April 2020 is a decisive turning point for British social democracy. Which political sage, a mere 12 months before, would have thought that a new Labour leader, with a party 'under new management' in Starmer's own words, would now be demonstrating a competence and potential electability that Labour has not offered the electorate since 2015 and before?

Yet, while the levers of power inside the party are gradually being prised from what proved to be the deadly and destructive Corbynista grasp, the nature of the Starmer 'project' for Labour's future remains ill-defined. In part, this is due to the exigencies of the COVID-19 emergency, which has overwhelmed the agenda of normal political discourse. In part, though, there is an understandable ambivalence about how much on policy Starmer should acknowledge or overturn of the Corbyn legacy.

Labour activists interpret this ambivalence in terms of the internal Labour politics of Starmer's successful leadership campaign. Starmer had to obtain the votes of large numbers of one-time Corbyn supporters among the party membership – Labour members, many new to the party, who once felt inspired by what they saw as the idealism and ethical socialist conviction of what Corbyn represented in the leadership elections of 2015 and 2016. The fresh hope of 'an honest, straightforward politics' that could bring about a radical break with the apparent timidity of the Labour establishment's response to austerity and rising inequality contrasted favourably with the decent but uninspiring offerings of his main leadership opponents.

Enthusiasm for Corbyn's politics was reinforced by the *apparent* electoral success of the 2017 manifesto in supposedly winning back support for Labour. Academic evidence is sceptical of this claim. At least as big a part was played by Theresa May's ineffective campaign. One might go further and describe the May campaign as disastrous, until one remembers that the Conservatives ended up with some 60 more seats in the Commons than Labour at this 'highpoint' of Corbyn popularity! It is an indisputable fact that in 2017, Labour benefited hugely from Liberal Democrat and Conservative 'Remain' supporters believing that a Labour vote was the least damaging of the available evils, especially as, the polling forecast correctly, there was never much chance of Jeremy Corbyn actually ending up as prime minister.

By the time of last December's general election, however, many Corbyn enthusiasts had become disillusioned by Labour's internal divisions over anti-Semitism and Europe. In the intervening period, Corbyn's credibility with the electorate had been gravely weakened by self-inflicted damaging episodes such as his reaction to the Salisbury poisonings, which proved publicly impactful and highly symbolic.

As a result, a crucial section of the Labour membership supported Starmer because they had become disillusioned not with the radical transformative change that they imagined Corbyn once promised, but with the baggage that seemingly dragged him down. They still supported the 'socialist' message but knew Labour needed a new message carrier with a more consensus-building style within the party and with the public. Of this 'socialist' message, the reinstatement of public ownership as a central objective of Labour policy was an important symbolic part.

In the leadership election campaign of early 2020, the Starmer campaign did not seek to question Labour's leftward turn. The ten policy pledges Starmer made summarised the essence of the two Corbyn manifestos. Under the heading 'Common ownership', Starmer stated: 'Public services should be in public hands, not making profits for shareholders. Support for common ownership of rail, mail, energy and water; end outsourcing in our NHS, local government and justice system.'[4] This statement is inadequate at several different levels. First, the tone of the language suggests that private ownership and profit is, by definition, opposed to the public good. Are airlines not public services? If profit seeking is opposed to the public good, why would one ever risk flying EasyJet on holiday! To suggest this is a major error that puts Labour outside the mainstream of European social democracy.

Second, in reality, there is not a 'sacred garden' of public services that can somehow be ring-fenced against the supposed evils of profit-making capitalism. Just think of the greatest health challenge of the day: a vaccine to defeat COVID-19. Our hopes rest on an effective partnership between the brilliance of publicly funded research and the innovative drive of private sector pharma companies. Frankly, in these circumstances, who will mind if the successful pharma companies make a decent profit?

Third, to rule out all outsourcing in the provision of public services is dogmatic and unjustified. I am no fan of *compulsory* outsourcing of public services. As a member of Cumbria County Council, I have seen the benefit of bringing formerly outsourced social care and children's services in-house. Private provision *can* be more expensive than public. Decent public sector pay and conditions *can* underpin the 'spirit of public service' that leads to higher-quality delivery. However, if a public service is being inefficiently provided, and internal change management fails to remedy the problems, then the potential for outsourcing should remain a matter for local democratic decision.

Fourth, Labour cannot propose a programme of renationalisation until it offers credible answers to legitimate questions about how its 2019 commitments would be financed. Labour needs clear principles, starting with 'value for money', by which all its actions will be judged. This will prove essential for electoral success in a post-COVID-19 world where public debt will be far higher than anything envisaged in Labour's 2017 and 2019 manifestos.

What do 'new times' demand? The need for an active, modern industrial policy

There is nothing shameful in being a pragmatist. I am not opposed to nationalisation in all circumstances. In the 2008 banking crisis, the nationalisation of Northern Rock, then Royal Bank of Scotland (RBS) and other banks, helped avert the collapse of the financial system that the US refusal to rescue Lehman Bros threatened. Without it, and comparable action in other countries, Britain and the world could have suffered a depression on the scale of the 1930s. It was the right and brave thing for Gordon Brown to do, and he is yet to win the credit in history for it.

It is also foolish to deny realities that stare one in the face. Rail privatisation has failed. The infrastructure has, in effect, been in public hands since the creation of Network Rail out of the collapse of Railtrack some 20 years ago. For the passenger operating companies, the franchise system is completely discredited: half the franchises are in quasi-public ownership because the holders proved unable to deliver the results they had promised. The best thing would be to reintegrate infrastructure and service provision in public hands, though there is room for debate about whether to retain the concept of an 'open network', supervised by a regulator, which would allow, at the margin, private companies to offer innovative freight and passenger services alongside the public system.

Is there a more general argument that public ownership and state intervention have become newly relevant to 'new times'? We must all remember, whatever our ideological starting points, the injunction memorably attributed to Keynes: 'If the facts change, I change my mind: what do you do, sir?' However, what facts might have changed to justify the return of public ownership to a central place in Labour's programme?

Some might cite: the need to halt the supposed 'privatisation' of the NHS; the scandal of privatised utility profits; the financial crisis of 2008 and the perceived failure of the banks to channel finance for investment to home-based companies; the need for national and regional investment banks to drive new growth in deindustrialised Britain; and the imperative for the public sector to be the driving force in the Green New Deal. There is some merit in all these points. To me, they argue for bespoke solutions to varied challenges that all require a stronger emphasis on effective public–private partnership and stronger market regulation. However, to argue on these grounds for nationalisation and public ownership on the post-Second World War model is neither necessary nor politically sensible.

Such a response is bound to be interpreted by Labour's opponents as a reversion to outdated left-wing dogma by a group of retro socialists bent on reversing the processes of social democratic modernisation that Neil Kinnock, John Smith and Tony Blair *all* persuaded the party to accept from the mid-1980s to the mid-1990s. The psephological evidence is overwhelming that it was this process of Labour modernisation, ridding itself of the hard Left and its uncompromising dogma, that laid the basis for Blair's three election victories and 13 years of, overall, highly successful Labour government.

Labour should commence a sensible debate about the balance sheet of those 13 years. Maybe Labour could have been bolder and achieved more transformative change, though in what areas? To write off these Labour years in government as no better than a Tory government is an outrageous libel and straight untruth. To put it provocatively, is Labour's failure to advance the cause of public ownership and nationalisation from 1997 to 2010 more important to the British Left than the establishment of the national minimum wage and stronger workplace rights based on the European Social Chapter, the dramatic reduction in child and pensioner poverty, the rescue and transformation of the NHS, the massive extension of educational opportunity, the foundation of Sure Start, the advances in social equality for women, black, Asian and minority ethnic (BAME) and LGBT citizens, and all the other major social advances that those Labour governments achieved? Surely not.

Yet, a legitimate critique of New Labour's decade in office from 1997 until the financial crisis is that the government underplayed the potential value of a modern industrial policy in enhancing UK competitiveness, addressing regional inequalities and stimulating decent, sustainable jobs for the future. As Secretary of State for Business from October 2008, Peter Mandelson reopened this policy agenda, though it came too late to rescue Labour electorally. It did however create a consensus for a bigger role for government in industrial strategy that was followed up by the Coalition and May governments, at least in conception, if not in a strong enough impetus for action.

Conclusion

Labour should now build on this consensus for a modern industrial policy. It should put alongside it a policy of more active labour market intervention to make a decisive break with the low-wage, low-skill equilibrium that dominates major sectors of UK employment. It should back an imaginative role for public equity stakes *in a new partnership with* (not opposition to) the private sector. In choosing its private sector partners, it should look to the suppliers of long-term patient capital, for example, in pension funds, not the City operators who are only interested in short-term financial engineering for maximum profit. Also, while it makes sense to retain a UK national strategy for research and key industrial sectors such as aerospace, automobiles and pharmaceuticals, the main thrust of industrial policy delivery should be through a real devolution of political and financial power across England, as well as to the nations of the UK. These are all points that Keir Starmer, as well as Ed Davey, should ponder in setting out a new progressive vision for the 2020s and beyond.

Notes

[1]   Early socialists were attracted to Radical ideas for nationalisation of the land. Many also backed public ownership of the mines

as the only means of improving the desperate conditions in the coal industry.

[2] Anthony Crosland (1956) *Future of Socialism*, London: Jonathan Cape Ltd.

[3] See 'UK Politics Blair practices football diplomacy with France', http://news.bbc.co.uk/1/hi/uk_politics/138475.stm

[4] Keir Starmer (2020) 'My pledges to you', 12 February. See https://keirstarmer.com/plans/10-pledges/

FIVE

How do we grow the economy without damaging the environment?

Dick Newby

In the aftermath of the Second World War, the aim of economic policy for a social democrat – and liberal – in the UK was simple. It could be summed up by the phrase 'full employment in a free society' – the title of William Beveridge's 1944 plan for a post-war world.

In 1945, the devastation caused by humankind was on itself, not other elements of the natural world. However, the success of Beveridge's ideas and Keynesian macroeconomic policies led to an unprecedented increase in per capita income, life expectancy and population. The figures are extraordinary. World population in 1950 was 2.5 billion. It is now 7.7 billion. Global life expectancy has increased from 46 to 71,[1] and income per head has increased from US$3,500 to US$17,000. No period in human history has seen such rapid and widespread increases. Furthermore, the world got used to the idea that economic growth – measured by gross domestic product (GDP) – would grow in developed countries by at least 2 per cent a year and in less developed countries by a lot more.

Growth was seen as desirable, not just because it increased the total stock of wealth and the flow of income, but because it offered the possibility of redistribution towards the poorer without requiring a fall in the absolute wealth and income of the most affluent. The benefits of growth, which included an enhanced welfare state and the provision of a large amount of social housing, could be channelled downwards. This idea permeated social democratic thought and was borne out by falling income inequality in the post-war period. It was a most benign scenario. Falling income inequality was only put into reverse when Margaret Thatcher used industrial strife and high inflation as pretexts to bear down on the public sector and laud everything private.

When doubts began to surface about whether such growth was compatible with the sustainability of the natural environment – as they did in the 1960s – they were pooh-poohed by most social democrats. When I spoke in a debate in the Oxford Union in 1972, arguing that environmental constraints could and should put a limit on growth, I was opposed by Professor Wilfred Beckerman of University College London, doyen of Labour Party economists, who tore into me on the basis that such ideas were middle-class whimsies and anathema to the interests of the working class, for whom growth was essential to improve their standards of living.

Although the environmental costs of growth were becoming clearer, it was not until 1987 that the Brundtland Commission produced the first influential argument for 'sustainable development', which it defined as a path of economic development whereby each generation leaves behind at least as large a stock of assets as it itself inherited. However, it took the first report of the Intergovernmental Panel on Climate Change (IPCC) in 1990, which showed how CO_2 emissions were raising global temperatures, to jolt decision-makers into taking sustainability seriously.

In the UK, a pivotal moment was the commissioning by Gordon Brown of the Stern Report on the Economics of Climate Change. Nick Stern, a social democrat himself, argued that, unchecked, climate change could lead to a loss of global GDP of 20 per cent or more and that increases of global temperatures of 5–6 degrees were a real possibility. This would have disastrous impacts on food production, human health and the environment. He argued that early action could more than justify the costs involved. Fast-forward, and the UK now has a legal requirement to reduce net CO_2 emissions by 2050 and a Committee on Climate Change tasked with setting out how that might be achieved.

Climate change is only one manifestation of how growth as we know it is unsustainable. Maintaining current living standards and economic systems already takes the resources of 1.7 earths.[2] In the past four decades, there has been a 60 per cent decline in the population of animals, birds and fish, and catastrophic rates of species extinction. The rate of extinctions continues to rise. As a result, the ecosystems on which human life depends – the Amazon basin, for example – are disappearing.

Against this background and the urgent necessity to move to a sustainable economy, using GDP as the principal measure of economic success is neither credible nor desirable. GDP has long been seen to be flawed – not least for failing to value many of the most important aspects of human behaviour, such as all forms of unpaid activity. It now fails because it completely ignores the depreciation of natural capital.

As we are now reaching the limits at which the earth can sustain growth using traditional production methods, we could only sustain indefinite GDP growth if the efficiency with which we can transform resources also increases indefinitely. Although we can still do a lot better on this – somewhere between 30 and 50 per cent of food produced is lost between farm and plate, for example – in the long run, it is impossible.

If GDP fails as a measure of growth in sustainable development, we need another measure. Cambridge economist Partha Dasgupta suggests that we should aim for 'inclusive wealth' to increase over time. Inclusive wealth includes not only traditional produced capital, but also natural capital and human capital (consisting of knowledge, education, health and skills). Under this measure, growth would consist of net domestic product (GDP less depreciation) minus aggregate consumption. It would be much less easy to compute than GDP, but it is probably the right target.

However, even without the sustainability imperative, traditional GDP growth is under threat because it simply is not happening. The assumption of consistent growth that has been valid in our lifetimes was shattered by the 2008 financial crisis, which resulted in the uninterrupted increase in personal income coming to a halt, or going into reverse, for millions in the UK and worldwide. Moreover, while its longer-term effects are unclear, COVID-19 is undoubtedly going to lead to lower growth and higher unemployment for a considerable period ahead. So, growth as we know it faces a double challenge: the future of humankind requires that we move to a sustainable economy; and our comfortable assumptions about consistent growth being an economic fact of life look obsolete.

Some people, of course, rejoice at the collapse of any sort of growth and argue that it was a false god in the first place. This view should not be ridiculed. J.S. Mill, writing in 1848, argued in favour of a stationary economy in order to promote 'mental culture, and moral and social progress'.[3] Keynes argued that 'the day is not far off when the economic problem will take the back seat where it belongs', being replaced by 'the problems of life and human relations, of creation and behaviour and religion'.[4]

Furthermore, in his path-breaking book *The Future of Socialism*, published in 1956, Anthony Crosland said that 'We stand on the threshold of mass abundance; and within a decade the average family will enjoy a standard of living which will convince the reformer that he should turn his main attention elsewhere' (that is, away from growth). Instead, while also advocating greater welfare and equality, he championed 'liberty and gaiety in private life' and 'culture and amenity planning'.[5]

Most recently, in his 2020 book *Slowdown: The End of the Great Acceleration – and why it's Good for the Planet, the Economy and Our Lives*, Professor Danny Dorling argues that far from growth spinning out of control, declines in fertility, population growth and technological change mean that it is possible that 'stability is not just possible, but that we are heading towards it'.[6] This sounds rather exaggerated but it appears to show that growth as we know it is finished. However, if we are to move towards a stable world in which humankind flourishes based on a new definition of growth, we must deal with the three challenges of achieving sustainability, becoming a fairer society and giving people something to aspire to going beyond material gain.

Achieving sustainability

In the UK, electricity generation fell by 16 per cent between 2005 and 2018, despite a 10 per cent increase in population and a 19 per cent rise in GDP.[7] However, of the Committee on Climate Change's 21 indicators of progress required to meet the net zero target by 2050, only four were on track. The committee's June 2020 report shows the successes (power generation and waste disposal), where the problem areas are (surface transport, buildings and agriculture) and how to deal with them. It is clear that failure to reach the targets would now largely be a failure of political will rather than lack of technical solutions.

Internationally, the picture is more mixed but many of the solutions exist – here are just three. First, stop subsidising the wrong things. Across the globe, subsidies exist that encourage consumption of fossil fuels, intensive agriculture, energy and fertilisers; these should end. Second, develop the circular economy, in which natural and manufactured resources used in the production of goods are reused and recycled using renewable power, so that resource inputs are minimised. Third, facilitate a reduction in population growth by making family planning accessible to all who want it – including an estimated 53 million women in Africa alone. Lack of political will by some of the world's leading economies – notably, the US and China – has been a major constraint; however, China's recent announcement to move to net zero by 2060 is now a significant step forward.

Becoming a fairer society

In *The Spirit Level*,[8] inequality of wealth and income has been shown to have negative impacts on societal goals such as social welfare, even ecological degradation, irrespective of absolute income levels. Moreover, if growth as we know it is dead, a tolerant, thriving society is only possible if its members believe that the same rules apply to everyone and they are fair.

To tackle these issues, we need tax justice, requiring wealthy individuals and companies to pay a fair share of tax that, at present, a combination of tax havens, money laundering, base erosion and profit shifting allows them to avoid. We need to shift taxation away from income towards wealth. This is much less evenly distributed: as Credit Suisse has pointed out, the richest 1 per cent own half the world's financial wealth.[9] We should guarantee basic universal social provision for everyone – and make the case for the tax increases that will inevitably be needed to fund this. To reduce the increase in unemployment that will be occasioned by COVID-19 in the short term, and the longer-term threat to jobs posed by AI, we should accelerate the investments needed to reach net zero in home insulation, battery and hydrogen production, public transport infrastructure, and zero-carbon house-building.

Conclusion: something to aspire to

As individuals, communities and a planet, we need to have something to which we can aspire, something that promises a better future and to which we can direct our energies – in short, a better life. Since Socrates, philosophers have speculated on what a better life might consist of – beyond having our basic needs of food, shelter and security catered for. Research by the New Economics Foundation has identified five key things that promote well-being: connecting to the people around us; being active in our bodies; taking notice of the world; learning new skills; and giving to others. How could these be turned more explicitly into public policy goals? We need to start at school and ensure that curiosity, empathy, creativity and an understanding of sustainability are as important as maths and English. We must also make it easier for people to develop their talents throughout their lives.

We should weave well-being into all public policies, and we should underpin all this by a piece of legislation building on the Future Generations Act, passed by the Welsh Parliament in 2015. This sets an overarching sustainability objective for government to be achieved by pursuing seven well-being goals, which include promoting a vibrant culture, a healthier population and cohesive communities in addition to prosperity, resilience, equality and global responsibility. Mill, Keynes and Crosland would approve.

The impossibility of indefinite economic growth, as traditionally defined, on a finite planet is now inescapable. For many, this will be a terrifying prospect – it requires economic theory and the assumptions of public policy to be ripped up.

However, it opens up the prospect of new goals for humankind that could increase well-being on a sustainable basis.

In an era of populist and authoritarian leaders, such a future will meet with fierce resistance. However, for social democrats and liberals, it is a future that really is worth fighting for.

Notes

[1] Max Roser (2018) 'Twice as long – life expectancy around the world', October, https://ourworldindata.org/life-expectancy-globally

[2] *The Guardian* (2018) 'Earth's resources consumed in ever greater destructive volumes', July, www.theguardian.com/environment/2018/jul/23/earths-resources-consumed-in-ever-greater-destructive-volumes

[3] John Stuart Mill (1909) *Principles of Political Economy*, Book IV, Chapter VI, London: Longmans, Green and Co. https://oll.libertyfund.org/titles/mill-principles-of-political-economy-ashley-ed

[4] First Annual Report of the Arts Council (1945–46) www.artscouncil.org.uk/arts-council-great-britain-1st-annual-report-1945

[5] Anthony Crosland (1956) *The Future of Socialism*, London: Jonathan Cape, 1956, pp 515 and 521.

[6] Professor Danny Dorling (2020) *Slowdown: The End of the Great Acceleration – and why it's Good for the Planet, the Economy and Our Lives*, New Haven & London: Yale University Press, pp 1–3.

[7] 'Analysis: UK electricity generation in 2018 falls to lowest level since 1994', January 2019, www.carbonbrief.org/analysis-uk-electricity-generation-2018-falls-to-lowest-since-1994

[8] Richard Wilkinson and Kate Pickett (2010) *The Spirit Level: Why Greater Equality Makes Societies Stronger*, New York: Bloomsbury Press.

[9] 'The 1% now own a staggering amount of the world's wealth – and it's proof inequality is worsening', businessinsider.com, November 2017, www.businessinsider.com/richest-1-own-over-half-the-worlds-wealth-2017-11

SIX

How can global free trade work for everyone?

Sarah Olney

Whatever else liberals and social democrats believe in, we believe in free trade. Free trade is more than just a tariff schedule or a list of commodity codes; it is a belief that individuals are more important than the state. It enables individuals to form economic relationships with each other, to transcend the restrictions of their background and nationalities, and to contribute what is best about themselves to the wider world. It enriches both sides – joining up demand with supply across national and geographic boundaries.

Free trade breaks down when national governments impose themselves between purchasers and suppliers, and demand some of the value of the transaction for themselves. It breaks down when established players in a domestic market use their greater leverage to protect their position against possible competitors. The forces undermining free trade – nationalism and vested interests – are precisely those that Liberal Democrats seek to combat.

So, it is no surprise that the pulse of liberalism first quickened to the issue of free trade. It is the founding narrative, the origin myth, the raison d'être and the rallying call around which the aristocratic Whigs, the Peelite Tories and the anti-Corn Law League Radicals united to form the Liberal Party, in opposition to the Tory Party of tariff reform and imperial preference.

The repeal of the Corn Laws represented a great strategic shift in UK economic policy. For the first time, cheaper prices for wage-earners were prioritised over higher prices for landowners, urban dwellers were favoured over rural and manufacturing was prioritised over agriculture. The consequence of cheaper food prices for the majority of the population meant greater disposable income, which, in turn, led to increased demand for manufactured goods. This boost to our domestic economy financed the huge leap forward in technology that Britain experienced in the second half of the 19th century, in terms of railways, motor cars, telephony and electrical power. Also, the increased status of ordinary working people was recognised by the gradual extensions to the voting franchise over the next 75 years. The contribution of working people to the wealth of the nation gave birth to the first social democratic movements – employers found it in their interests to provide decent housing and healthcare to their workers, and workers organised their own education and welfare systems.

Small wonder, then, that free trade has assumed an almost mythic status for those who believe in a liberal economy. However, the flag-wavers for free trade in the current age are just as likely to be right-wing Conservatives, touting the benefits of leaving the EU, as they are to be Liberal Democrats, singing the hymn of internationalism. Are we both talking about the same thing?

It is important to remember that for the Victorians, 'free trade' took place in a world that they largely controlled. It was easy enough to find new markets for British products when those countries were administered by the British, and there is a marked strand of imperial nostalgia in Conservative advocacy of free trade: a seeming belief that it was the inherent greatness of our Britishness that made us an economic power across the world for so many years. The theory goes that our membership of a protectionist bloc has constrained and diminished that power: the British light has been hidden under an EU bushel for 40 years and is now uncovered, ready to illuminate the world once more.

However, for modern liberals, free trade emphasises almost the exact opposite. Trade is a two-way transaction, and successful trading environments value both participants equally. Since the dismantling of the European empires, and the end of the Second World War, there have been decades of painstaking negotiations to build multilateral trading partnerships. Barriers have been slowly dismantled, shared interests have been built upon and mutual standards have been agreed. For Liberal Democrats, free trade means removing the additional costs imposed by rivalry, mistrust and conflict.

The value of a trading bloc is the ability to set common standards for all participants. Non-tariff barriers such as these are increasingly becoming more relevant as tariffs themselves become less prevalent. Common standards are the key to breaking down international trade barriers and enabling new entrants to markets. A standard set of regulations, agreed by national governments, can remove a great deal of checking and sampling for sellers and processors; anything produced to a certified standard will be guaranteed to be suitable for the purpose it is needed for, regardless of where it has been produced or by whom. The purchaser is free to distinguish just by price, availability and ease of transport. So, far from being an obstacle to trade, trading regulations can be key to accessing a much larger customer base for new entrants to the market.

A complaint levelled against the EU during the 2016 referendum campaign was that it had ceased to be a trading bloc and had morphed into a political superstate, laying down regulations on a host of non-trade matters that amounted to an undermining of national sovereignty. It was a reflection of the extent to which establishing a common set of trading principles can reach into every part of our daily lives. Employment rights, measures to protect the environment, animal welfare – the need to ensure that goods from different countries can compete equally in a cross-border market creates a requirement to reach back-up supply chains and impose order on a far greater range of activity than just the trading of goods.

However, the advantage of this extension of cross-border powers is that it created a framework for countries to work together to resolve issues that transcend national borders, for example, climate change, organised crime and tax evasion. National sovereignty is undermined to a much greater extent by these threats than it is by international cooperation to combat them. An increasingly digital and globalised world no longer recognises national borders, and the forces unleashed by new technology can no longer be controlled by single nations working alone.

Liberal free trade, therefore, requires cooperation between nations to an extent that goes far beyond product specifications. The limits of such an approach, however, are that decisions are made between national governments or delegated to officials; the mandates for and influences on this decision-making is obscure. However well-intentioned the measure, and however much broad consensus among delegates there may be, without the daylight that proper scrutiny by democratically elected representatives brings, the decisions appear to lack legitimacy in the eyes of members of the public. In the UK, at least, the founding of the European Parliament does not appear to have been sufficient to overcome this democratic deficit. The lesson of this experience is surely that, given the impact that trade deals and negotiating mandates can have on so many areas of life, proper democratic endorsement of approaches to trade must be fundamental.

The revived nationalism of the UK and US is threatening the liberal interpretation of free trade, which has held sway for 70 years. The US is responding to China's increase in economic power, which threatens its ability to dictate the terms of global trade, and the UK is responding to what 52 per cent of its citizens perceived to be an overreach of sovereignty by the EU.

Since the Second World War, the US has been the ultimate guarantor of the world order, of trade, as in much else. However,, not long after they defeated their rival military superpower and ended the Cold War, they faced a new economic rival in China. The particular challenge that China represents is that their economic gains are underpinned – to some extent – by the authoritarian regime that controls it. There are undoubtedly many economic benefits for countries everywhere to leverage from the rising incomes of 1.4 billion citizens. However, we cannot cede leadership of the international order to a country with as appalling a human rights record and lack of democracy as China. To look the other way on these issues while deferring to their greater economic muscle would be to effectively say that morality is relative – that the wealth in an economy can be uncoupled from the people who create it.

A global free trade policy must be one where individuals and their business interests can join up internationally without interference from their nations or governments. Where individual activities are curtailed or artificially limited by national government, there is no free trade. National governments must limit engagement with nations that cannot guarantee the freedom and safety of their own citizens. Economic gains built on exploitation, persecution or oppression are not sustainable.

The fundamental principle that should underpin global free trade is that it benefits individuals and sustains their freedom and livelihoods. As we strike new free trade agreements, we should set our face against deals that boost political parties or governments at the expense of the people.

It is easy for liberals to scoff at nationalism and to deride defensive measures aimed solely at protecting domestic markets, especially if these industries are internationally uncompetitive. However, sometimes this is done to protect jobs in a specific city or region; sometimes for less tangible reasons, like preserving a sense of place or national/regional pride. We overlook this at our peril. One of the lessons of Brexit was the extent to which millions of British people felt that 'Brussels' was telling provincial towns and cities that their communities and industries were worthless. One by one, our heavy industries have moved away to cheaper, more productive parts of the world, leaving the communities that used to serve them bereft of purpose. If we reach back further, to the 1980s, we can see a similar reaction to Thatcherism among the striking miners. Thatcher could only see that British mines were making losses; the miners saw (correctly) that closing mines would rip the hearts out of their communities.

Reflecting upon the lessons of the last few years can point us to the way ahead for a better version of free trade. In reaching out to international partners, we must not neglect the communities that create the goods and services we want to sell to the world, and the extent to which local pride is embedded within their creation. The underlying philosophy of free trade is comparative advantage – that Britain has the ability to manufacture certain products to a higher quality than other nations – and this advantage is rooted in our geography. There is a reason why the bitterest trade battles are fought over food products – they are products of distinctive landscapes, representing strong regional identities.

The future for free trade is not nationalistic, defensive trade policies, but to foster that sense of pride in our country, in its history, its geography and its people, in order to build up our key industries and focus on exporting. We need to identify which industries we are truly competitive in, nurture our domestic workforce to develop the key skills required to help them thrive and send those exports out into the world with a real sense that 'Made in Britain' can mean something again.

Two industries spring to mind. First, we have our creative industries. Our nation has produced some of the world's finest creative minds and continues to do so. Visual art, literature, music and drama – why are we not making the most of whatever strange alchemy exists between this landscape and its people by training more of our young people on instruments, in composition, in painting and in drawing? As we are better at these things than practically every nation on earth, they should all be central to our curriculum, accompanied by skilled training in the technologies that support them, from camera operators to bookbinders.

Second, we have led the world in zero-carbon technology, from energy generation to transport. Our carbon-emitting industries will not deliver sustainable growth – global demand for motor cars and petroleum will slowly fall over the next century as the world runs out of fossil fuels. We need to be on the front foot in developing the next generation of technology. We did it in the 19th century and we are well placed to do it again.

In 2020, the word 'transition' is most often used to refer to the UK's transition out of the EU. However, it is also being used by economists to talk about the world's movement away from carbon-emitting industries and practices – the transition towards net zero. It should also be an important word for national governments in their economic planning. How can we transition the people and communities that are engaged in industries with limited prospects towards those that have a more sustainable future? The key to our success in international trade lies in strengthening the communities of our towns and villages with the right skills to sustain the best of our British industries.

Conclusion

Liberal Democrats of both traditions have long believed in a form of free trade that benefits individuals, rather than governments, with reduced prices and the creation of new employment opportunities in the UK, while also benefiting people who live in the countries we trade with. Measures to create common standards, combined with other powers, can also bring improved employment rights, prevent non-tariff barriers from being used to stifle trade and allow action on issues that a single country cannot resolve, such as climate change, tax evasion and cross-border crime.

This is threatened by the rise of authoritarian states, which promote trade barriers as a form of nationalism and stir up suspicion of international cooperation. The lack of democratic accountability for international agreements has weakened the liberal and social democratic case for free trade. Making trade negotiations more accountable is vital to address this, and will open up to scrutiny any trade agreements with countries that abuse human rights.

Free trade can damage communities if their main employers are unable to survive in competition with international rivals. Two key areas where we have a comparative advantage are our creative industries and zero-carbon technology. The key to our success in international trade is developing skills required to thrive in areas such as these.

SEVEN

Towards a social democratic foreign policy?

Julie Smith

Ours will strive for Britain to be shed of all isolationist and xenophobic attitudes towards the management of our nation's foreign affairs. Hence, we support Britain's responsibilities within the European Economic Community, North Atlantic Treaty Organisation, the United Nations and the Commonwealth. Ours will commit Britain to become a constructive and progressive force within these trans-national bodies – in order to meet the challenges faced by the modern global community, such as arms control and third world poverty. We whole-heartedly reject the isolationist tendencies which dominate the Labour Party today.[1]

These words formed the core of a set of foreign policy ideals that drew the author as a schoolgirl to the embryonic Social Democrats. They outlined a vision for the UK's role in the world that was collaborative, not competitive, and that understood the importance of multilateral institutions and the rules-based international order. They rejected isolationism and unilateralism, on the one hand, and jingoism, on the other. They implicitly acknowledged that the world had moved on from the Empire and that Britannia no longer ruled the waves, but they provided enough vision to begin to respond to Dean Acheson's immortal words: 'Britain has lost an Empire and not yet found a role.'[2] The language may now seem somewhat dated, the Labour Party may no longer be isolationist, but at a time when the forces of populism and isolation have led to the abandonment of treaties and international law, the values of the Limehouse Declaration are even more vital than ever.

Four decades ago, the SDP was born in the midst of deep divisions, both political and economic, within the UK. The political landscape saw right-wing conservatism trouncing an increasingly left-wing Labour Party. The SDP appeared to offer something of a middle way, embracing aspects of capitalism but recognising that the state had an important role to play in creating social justice. As in economics, so in foreign policy: Social Democrats steered a middle course, supporting a strong defence and being willing to intervene internationally to pursue progressive policies or overturn injustice, while eschewing narrow nationalism.

As domestic politics polarised, so did parties' foreign policy preferences. The difference was at its starkest during the 1983 general election. The Labour Party favoured rejecting key Western alliances: it pledged to leave the North Atlantic Treaty Organisation (NATO) and the European Economic Community (as the EU was then known), and advocated unilateral nuclear disarmament. Meanwhile, the Conservatives focused on a strong defence, rather than an internationalist policy. Like the Liberals, with whom they would soon ally and then merge, Social Democrats advocated internationalism. The Limehouse Declaration even used the language of 'responsibility', not as a neocolonial power, but as a member of a wide array of multilateral institutions forged in the wake of two disastrous world wars. The emergent Social Democrats chose neither the jingoism espoused by some in the Conservative Party, as exemplified by Margaret Thatcher in reclaiming the Falkland Islands, nor the unilateralism verging on pacifism of the Labour Party.[3] Rather, they endorsed an avowedly multilateral approach to foreign policy and defence.

In particular, Social Democrats (like their Liberal allies) were passionate in their support for European integration, not for idealistic or ideological reasons (though, of course, such reasons played a part in the thinking of certain individuals), nor yet for some unfathomable, ideological belief in institutions for their own sake, but for the perceived benefits membership brought. Working collectively with neighbours and other countries that hold similar values – the 'like-minded' as Ed Davey referred to them when he was Secretary of State for Energy and Climate Change, and now a commonly used term – can enhance resilience and strengthen security in one's own country and that of other member states.

The international context was to change fundamentally in the decade after the Limehouse Declaration, as the Cold War ended, a divided European continent unified and 'history ended', according to Francis Fukuyama at least. There were calls for a 'peace dividend' and defence budgets were slashed in the UK, as elsewhere. The raisons d'être of certain post-war international institutions came into question but they ultimately persisted, and even thrived in the case of the EU, though NATO's role is perhaps more contested. Furthermore, if some of the Cold War threats had ended, intractable foreign policy challenges remained, not least as Russia, now a direct geographical neighbour to the EU and NATO, proved reluctant to espouse the democratic norms favoured by the West. Their values were simply too incompatible, and as NATO expanded, the Russian response showed that Europe faced more dangers, not fewer. The pursuit of a 'peace dividend' ensured fewer resources were available after the Cold War to finance defence in the UK and NATO more broadly. Collaboration and pooling of resources thus became more important than ever for the UK's foreign policy and defence.

Of course, one might query why social democrats would favour a strong defence policy, then or now. What role should one state play in the affairs of others? Is it possible for a country to export its values? Should we seek to do so? The EU has certainly tried to do so via the conditionality associated with its enlargement policy, including adherence to the human rights regime of the Council of Europe and the associated European Convention on Human Rights.[4] Foreign policy can be seen as an expression of wider social democratic values, including democracy, human rights and the rule of law. All are values that social democrats would support, whether at home or abroad. The same is true of social justice. Yet, while it became commonplace in the immediate aftermath of the Cold War to fight for such values at home and in many former communist states that turned to so-called Western values and institutions, what is the rationale for doing so in foreign policy? At its simplest, it is the duty of the state to protect its citizens, and a credible military capability can prove a strong deterrent. A more complex answer, and one that better explains wider social democratic foreign policy, would be that evil exists that states may need to be prepared to oppose. Military capabilities are an important part of a state's metaphorical armoury, all of which combine to allow international intervention for limited purpose, typically for humanitarian reasons, and certainly not for aggressive reasons or in search of territorial expansion.

Questions of social justice cannot easily be confined within national borders and some injustices necessitate intervention. Starvation and human rights abuses, especially genocide, are all phenomena that should be tackled regardless of where they occur. This is the reason for the social democratic commitment to use international development aid to reduce poverty, as opposed to using it to further the UK's national interest. This is perhaps one of the clearest distinctions in the 2020s between Liberal Democrats and the Conservative Party. In coalition, the two parties worked to enshrine the long-standing global target of 0.7 per cent of gross national product (GNP) for development aid into law. It was clearly a Liberal Democrat-led initiative but one that the moderates within the Conservative Party under David Cameron willingly accepted: aid was seen as valuable in and of itself, without any formal links to trade and narrow national interest. The shift under the Johnson government is remarkable – with the right wing of his party in the ascendant, a dramatic reabsorption of the Department for International Development (DfID) into the Foreign and Commonwealth Office (FCO) and demands that aid support the UK's national interest, the balance between trade, aid, foreign policy and defence has changed fundamentally.

Of course, these aspects of international policy are interrelated; no one would suggest otherwise. Well-targeted international aid can help create and foster resilient local economies, reducing some of the factors leading to conflict or failed/failing states. Aid may reduce the need for other tools of international policy later. Averting conflict is clearly preferable to responding to conflict in terms of the lives of the communities affected and the costs of military intervention, both financial and in terms of potential lives lost. At times, military intervention may be required.[5] When that is the case, the purpose of engagement should be clear and limited, and an exit strategy should be determined in advance, in line with humanitarian intervention under the doctrine of the 'Responsibility to Protect'.[6] Such an approach was taken in 2000 with the military intervention in Sierra Leone by the 'New' Labour government, which, in many ways, could be seen to embody aspects of social democracy, two decades after the foundation of the SDP. In contrast, the 2003 invasion of Iraq failed to follow this doctrine.

Conclusion

Social democratic foreign policy was and remains pragmatic but values-driven. It eschews jingoism and calls to 'go global' for reasons of narrow national self-interest. It favours a foreign policy that provides security for the nation's citizens and expansion of social justice across the world. In this very real sense, all lives matter, irrespective of geography, in the sense that national borders should not determine whether fundamental human rights are respected. Enhancing the life chances of people in the developing world matters to those individuals who are helped but, more fundamentally, whole communities can benefit, paving the way for more resilient societies. When fragile economies are stabilised, those nations will be strengthened, thereby reducing the risk of more wholesale intervention down the line.

International aid has become a contentious issue in British politics, with the tabloid press railing against 'our' money being sent abroad. The trope that was used to vilify the financial costs of membership of the EU has been repurposed to criticise the UK's international development budget. This hostility was already the case before the 2016 referendum and is shared by a large section of the parliamentary Conservative Party, not to mention many voters. While the decision to bring DfID back into the FCO was supposed to strengthen the UK's global reach and not reduce development spending, the economic impact of the COVID-19 crisis inevitably reduces the size of the development budget and, hence, its effectiveness. This risks a further backlash from citizens who have been particularly hard hit by the economic consequences of COVID-19 in the UK. Leadership is required if the UK is to continue to play the leading role in international development for which it is so respected, and it certainly is not coming from the Conservative Party.

In many ways, the 2019 general election seemed to hark back to the 1980s: Labour was led by a veteran Eurosceptic, who had long opposed the nuclear deterrent, while under Brexit-touting Boris Johnson, the Conservatives were promising to 'go global' – a vacuous term but one that has a strong tinge of jingoism. The key change on the Tory side was a move away from the European cause. 'Get Brexit done' was the prevailing discourse in the Conservatives' electorally successful campaign. Initially successful in his own terms of taking the UK out of the EU, the Prime Minister will eventually find that negotiating the UK's longer-term relations with the EU will be more difficult. The sight of the Tories ripping up the rule book (literally and metaphorically) and threatening to break international law demonstrated just how fragile the UK's internal political order has become. The threat of breaching international law raises deep concerns – the ensuing breach of trust will render the UK's attempts to forge future alliances increasingly difficult. Trashing the rules-based international order is not the way to win friends or influence people. The direction of travel for the UK under the Johnson government is one that liberals and social democrats alike must view with horror.

Some 40 years on, the values enshrined in the Limehouse Declaration are more important than ever. The Labour Party is no longer led by a unilateralist, so it is now the time for social democrats to bridge the divide and work together on foreign policy goals. A failure to do so could leave the UK fundamentally diminished, no longer able to garner the trust and cooperation of other nations that are so vital in an interdependent world.

Notes

[1] The Limehouse Declaration (1981) The full text of the Limehouse Declaration can be found here: https://poluk.fandom.com/wiki/Limehouse_Declaration

[2] Dean Acheson, speech at the Military Academy, West Point, 5 December 1962. See https://www.oxfordreference.com/view/10.1093/acref/9780191843730.001.0001/q-oro-ed5-00000015

[3] Here, many Social Democrats would part company with some of their Liberal allies, who were less likely to accept the logic of multilateralism – a difference of opinion that can still be seen in the party more than 30 years after merger.

[4] Equality and Human Rights Commission, 'What is the European Convention on Human Rights?', www.equalityhumanrights.com/en/what-european-convention-human-rights

[5] See Policy Exchange (2017) 'The Cost of Doing Nothing: The price of inaction in the face of mass atrocities', https://policyexchange.org.uk/wp-content/uploads/2017/01/Intervention-01-17_v8.pdf. The paper was written by Conservative MP Tom Tugendhat and Labour MP Alison McGovern, building on the work of the late Jo Cox MP, demonstrating how such considerations can resonate across the political divide.

[6] United Nations Office on Genocide and Responsibility to Protect, 'Responsibility to Protect', www.un.org/en/genocideprevention/about-responsibility-to-protect.shtml

EIGHT

How do we deliver social justice through education?

Stephen Williams

England and Wales have now had 150 years of state education. Various reforms since the Gladstone government's 1870 Act have undoubtedly transformed the life chances of millions of people. Yet, some aspects have changed little, the emphasis being still mainly academic, not vocational. Social mobility is possible but Gladstone's current successor is yet another old Etonian. Britain, especially England, is still a country where your life chances are set at birth. While being born privileged in Britain means that you are likely to remain privileged, if you are born disadvantaged, then you have to overcome a series of barriers to ensure that you and your children are not stuck in the same trap.[1]

The top echelons of British society are still viewed through a glass ceiling by most of us. Our education system must be the means to shatter it. We also have a sticky floor of underachievement holding back a stubbornly consistent fifth of our young people who fail to reach the minimum standards of literacy and numeracy essential to survive in the modern world. Again, our education system must be the means to allow people to rise. It is time for some real 'levelling up'.

To thrive in the next fifth of the 21st century, Britain will need a skilled workforce to attract investors away from our EU neighbours. We need our people to be flexible, creative and entrepreneurial. We must have the skills to design and develop world-beating products and services. Our education system and its outcomes must be changed in order to meet this challenge. According to education statistics produced by the OECD club of richer countries, Britain is just about inside the top third of its members on measurements of average literacy and numeracy scores. We are in the same cohort as the US, Japan and Sweden but we are far behind Canada, Korea and Poland, and other countries are likely to overtake us.[2]

Britain's average scores are held down by the bottom fifth of our young people, a tail of underachievers. Most but not all of them are from disadvantaged families. It is this group of people who are failed the most by our education system. The OECD found that 17 per cent of 15 year olds did not reach the Level 2 minimum standard of literacy, with 19 per cent failing to attain functional numeracy. Many of them would be from disadvantaged homes but 14 per cent of disadvantaged children actually reached the highest standards. Disadvantage need not determine destiny for everyone.

The most widely used measure of disadvantage is eligibility for free school meals (FSM). In England, the meals are claimed by approximately 2 million children, about 27 per cent of the

5–16 eligible age group.[3] In 2018, there was a 22 per cent gap in the Key Stage 2 expected standards for reading, writing and maths for 11 year olds between children on FSM and their classmates from more advantaged homes. At GCSE level, the gap was similar, with only 40 per cent of 16 year olds on FSM gaining a grade 4 (a C in the previous system) or above in English and maths compared with 68 per cent for their more advantaged peers.[4] The FSM statistics might have been even worse but for the disreputable practice of 'off-rolling' by some secondary schools, that is, failing to enter children for exams who are likely to fail, in order to inflate the school's headline results.

The Education Policy Institute measures the attainment gap in terms of the number of months disadvantaged children are behind their classmates. At age 16, they estimate that persistently disadvantaged children are a stark 22 months behind. At current rates of progress, it will take decades to close the gap.[5]

This must be considered an education emergency by all policymakers. It is not just our economic performance that is being held back; rather, the least skilled are the most likely to be in prison and have poor public health outcomes. A society is also more liberal and socially just the more its people are educated enough to not fear diversity, difference and challenging times.

Just as depressing is the way high-achieving young people from disadvantaged backgrounds are still held back later in life. About a quarter of people who were on FSM go on to university, still well behind the 43 per cent of more advantaged young people who enter higher education – the gap has changed little in the last 15 years – but only 5 per cent of students on FSM enter the most highly selective universities.[6] This means that the best-paid jobs and the most influential positions in society go largely to people from far more privileged backgrounds. A study by the Sutton Trust in 2016 showed that just over half of journalists had attended private schools. The proportions rose to 61 per cent for medicine and 71 per cent for barristers.[7] British society is still dominated by an elite who have little comprehension of what it means to be frustrated by poverty and feel that life is like pushing a boulder up a hill.

The situation in politics is similar, with very few people from poor or just ordinary backgrounds rising to the levels where decisions are made, including the critical ones about education policy. As well as an attainment chasm, we have a power gap between those from poor backgrounds and the people who have their hands on the levers of power and influence.

We need a radical shift in our education system to challenge and disrupt the elite so that the disadvantaged break through the glass ceiling. The system must also change to enable the disadvantaged to break free from the sticky floor that holds them back. Here are my eight suggestions of ways to make a step change.

First, the school *curriculum* must be inclusive and relevant. Young people must be prepared for the real-world challenges that they will face in the next decade. Britain's economy will have been damaged by Brexit and COVID-19. The pace of economic change will be unrelenting as we respond to climate change, automation of work and other technological advances. Change need not be alarming if the curriculum is flexible and responsive to a rapidly changing world. We need our young people to be world-ready, not just exam-ready.

The Coalition and subsequent Conservative governments made major changes to the GCSE examinations. Attainment is now measured across nine numbered grades, with a grade 9 being at the top level of the former A*. The GCSE curriculum has also been reformed, with an emphasis on academic rigour and preparation for university. This very obviously fails the majority of young people who will not progress to higher education. Student success will eventually be measured for award of an English Baccalaureate,[8] showing attainment in eight subjects (maths, English language and literature, three sciences, a language, and either history or geography) that have a whiff of ministerial nostalgia rather than preparing students for their working lives and personal challenges in the middle decades of the century. While it is possible for students to study art, design, music or drama, no recognition will be given to the school for attainment in those subjects. This means the curse of perverse league-table incentives will have more potency.

Creativity and innovation must be given more value when assessing attainment. Life skills (rather than 'soft skills') should also be fostered in school. Team working, problem solving and communication skills are more relevant to success in life than memorising quotes from Shakespeare. Even if an author inspires the use of language, confidence in speaking and writing compellingly are essential skills in life. As well as the traditional 3Rs, we need a fourth one: articulation.

Subjects in the core curriculum should also be made more relevant to the lives of pupils. Maths should be as much about financial literacy as solving equations. History should be about understanding our diverse society, not a list of the doings of rich, white, straight men. Personal, social and health education should be compulsory in every state school. An inclusive and relevant curriculum would be of more interest and relevance to pupils, having a positive impact on attainment as well as preparedness for life.

The successful delivery of any curriculum is down to the *teachers* in the classroom. The quality of any education system cannot exceed the quality of its teachers.[9] We must raise the esteem of the teaching profession, making it an attractive career for the brightest graduates. The best teachers must be deployed in the schools where they can make the most difference to the life chances of the disadvantaged. This will require intervention into the job market, where there are about 25,000 individual school employers, half-a-million qualified teachers and a national pay scale.

There are already plans to raise starting salaries in 2022 to £30,000[10] and a job market for new graduates disrupted by COVID-19 may also attract more people into the safer economic haven of teaching. Bursaries also exist for shortage subjects at secondary level. An extra incentive should be offered to attract the best teachers to low-attaining local authority areas or to particular schools anywhere with a history of low attainment for poorer pupils. The salary supplement should be funded centrally, not from the school budget.

Pupil premium money[11] could be used to buy in specialist tutors for disadvantaged children, giving them access to the burgeoning market of top-up home tutoring that is now common for many children from middle-class families. High-achieving teachers should be offered term or whole-year sabbaticals to attend a National Centre of Education Excellence to share their own and learn best practice from other teachers.

The *schools inspection* regime is being reformed but I would like to see a particular emphasis on checking the effectiveness of a school in raising the attainment of its pupils who qualify for pupil premium, those with a statement of special educational needs and those with a caring responsibility at home. This would include schools currently rated outstanding, which are exempt from inspection.

Children from disadvantaged backgrounds can be found in every school. This was the reason for the Liberal Democrat policy of awarding the pupil premium for each child on FSM or in care. There are, however, huge variations between schools in the proportion of children on FSM. Many 'comprehensive' schools are nothing of the sort, having a very unbalanced social intake. This is particularly noticeable in large urban areas, where the 'best' schools often have very low numbers of children on FSM, compared to the average number across the town or city. Much of this can be explained by the economics of the local housing market, with huge premiums on homes in close proximity to a school with good results. Children on FSM should not be effectively denied access to the best schools in their city because their parents cannot afford to live in a desirable area. The *admissions code* should stipulate that in urban areas where a different school choice is practicable, all schools (including faith schools) should have an FSM intake broadly equivalent to the local authority or city average. A comprehensive intake is good for social cohesion as well as attainment.

The logical extension of a fair admissions code is an *end to academic selection*. There are only 163 grammar schools remaining in England.[12] They educate approximately 176,000 pupils, the vast majority from better-off families. It is time to end the political cowardice that enables this indulgence.

It would be illiberal to advocate the abolition of the main source of education privilege: private fee-paying schools. However, it is an absurdity that just over a thousand of them claim charitable status[13] when there is little evidence of them providing public benefit on a wide or fair basis. They should be offered the chance of joining the state family of schools as independent academies. Bristol Cathedral School and Colston's Girls School took this route a decade ago and have seen a big expansion in their pupil numbers. Those that decline should lose their charitable status and pay business rates,[14] VAT on their fees and taxes on their often-considerable investment income. The glass ceiling would become thinner, even if it did not shatter.

The pupil premium stops at year 11, the year most pupils take GCSEs, despite students in school sixth forms being eligible for FSM. At this age, many students from disadvantaged backgrounds are found in further education colleges. A *student premium* should be introduced to enable schools and colleges to continue the support already given up until GCSE level. The premium should support students whether they are studying for A level, the new vocational T level or a Level 3 apprenticeship so that they make the best possible university or career choices.

The introduction of a student premium for 16–18 year olds should enable the development of a system to track young people from disadvantaged backgrounds. As well as the obvious use for assessing the effectiveness of policies, it would also enable universities to work with schools to identify potential students in order to ensure fair access to the most selective institutions.

A more radical change to the admissions system would also increase the likelihood of fair access, with a switch to *post-qualification applications*. The August 2020 A level results fiasco exposed the long-standing problem of potential students and universities matching each other when the final grade is not known for certain. Institutional convenience and academic conservatism are no excuse for not changing the date of university admissions to a time when the final grades are known. Students would then know their true worth and potential. It would end the increasing practice of unconditional offers, which may actually be depressing student attainment. High-achieving students from disadvantaged backgrounds could be snapped up by the most exclusive universities. They would go on to be the leaders of society, building a fairer and more successful Britain.

Conclusion

Achieving social justice is the aspiration that unites social democrats, whichever political party they support. Britain is a long way from being a socially just country. It is unacceptable that about a fifth of our young people fail to reach the minimum standards expected at the end of their time in school. This is the longest period when the state has the most direct influence on their lives. It lets them down and must do far better. Education is the clearest path to a fulfilling life. Our schools must offer an inclusive curriculum that addresses the real-life challenges that young people will face. The brightest graduates need to be offered a rewarding career in teaching, where they will be able to make a transformational difference to the life chances of the children from disadvantaged backgrounds. The state should not just give a firm helping hand to lift people up from the sticky floor that holds them back; it must also remove the barriers and clear the obstacles that stand in the way of people from poorer backgrounds reaching the top of our main professions and institutions. Education must be the way to achieve a genuinely meritocratic society where no one is held back purely by the circumstances of their birth.

Notes

[1] Social Mobility Commission (2019) 'State of the nation 2018–19, social mobility in Great Britain', April, www.gov.uk/government/publications/social-mobility-in-great-britain-state-of-the-nation-2018-to-2019

[2] OECD (2019) 'PISA 2018 results', www.oecd.org/pisa/Combined_Executive_Summaries_PISA_2018.pdf

[3] House of Commons Library (2020) 'Pupil premium', February, https://commonslibrary.parliament.uk/research-briefings/sn06700/

[4] Social Mobility Commission (2019) 'State of the nation 2018–19, social mobility in Great Britain', April, Figures 3.2 and 3.3, www.gov.uk/government/publications/social-mobility-in-great-britain-state-of-the-nation-2018-to-2019

[5] Education Policy Institute (2019) 'Annual report', https://epi.org.uk/publications-and-research/annual-report-2019/. The pupil premium is awarded to pupils who have been in receipt of FSM

at any point in the last six years, the 'ever 6 group'. The tighter group of persistently disadvantaged children constitutes those that have been on FSM for 80 per cent of their time in school.

[6] Social Mobility Commission (2019) 'State of the nation 2018–19, social mobility in Great Britain', April, ch 5, www.gov.uk/government/publications/social-mobility-in-great-britain-state-of-the-nation-2018-to-2019

[7] Sutton Trust (2016) 'Leading people', www.suttontrust.com/wp-content/uploads/2019/12/Leading-People_Feb16-1.pdf. Sutton Trust (2019) 'Elitist Britain', www.suttontrust.com/wp-content/uploads/2019/12/Elitist-Britain-2019.pdf

[8] House of Commons Library (2019) 'English Baccalaureate', September, https://commonslibrary.parliament.uk/research-briefings/sn06045/

[9] Angel Gurría, OECD Secretary-General, 'PISA 2009 Results: What Makes a School Successful?', www.oecd.org/pisa/pisaproducts/48852721.pdf

[10] House of Commons Library (2019) 'Teacher recruitment and retention', December, https://commonslibrary.parliament.uk/research-briefings/cbp-7222/

[11] The pupil premium was a Liberal Democrat policy introduced by the Coalition government in 2011. Schools in England are awarded extra funds for each pupil in receipt of FSM or in care. The 2020 values are £1,345 at primary level and £955 for secondary-age children. Smaller amounts are also available for the children of armed forces personnel. In 2020, the total cost was £2.4 billion.

[12] House of Commons Library (2020) 'Grammar school statistics', January, https://commonslibrary.parliament.uk/research-briefings/sn01398/

[13] House of Commons Library (2019) 'Charitable status and independent schools', October, https://commonslibrary.parliament.uk/research-briefings/sn05222/

[14] The Scottish government abolished business rates relief for private schools in March 2020.

NINE

What is the Social Democrat Group?

Colin McDougall and George Kendall

If we social democrats believe in pragmatic ways to deliver social justice, we need to have our existing views challenged. The Social Democrat Group does not just tolerate different views, but seeks them out.

This is reflected in the book, for example, there are different views on universal basic income, and a piece warning of the dangers of growth to the environment, but another warning of the dangers to prosperity by impeding international trade. The group aims to stimulate debate and contribute to the centre-left finding a way to navigate these conflicting priorities.

Roger Liddle's piece is very welcome. It is a fascinating read, based on detailed expertise and experience, and reminds sensible Labour and Liberal Democrats how much in common we have. The Social Democrat Group has always sought to reach out to social democrats beyond the Liberal Democrats. We must continue to do so, and so contribute to a wider movement to get rid of this awful government. The following are some reasons that our Executive members believe the Social Democrat Group is important.

Michael Mullaney – Vice-chair

As a local councillor in Hinckley and Bosworth in Leicestershire, I am part of a local team that managed to win control of the council last May in a massively Leave area (60+ per cent) by concentrating on the day-to-day issues that affected people's lives. In our literature and online, we campaigned on the need: for improved local health and education services; for protecting local rural bus services and improving rail services; and for protecting vital local services, such as Sure Start Children's Centres and libraries.

On a national level, however, we found it much more difficult to convince people to vote for us as our national messages often concentrated on Europe, or on other issues that people did not see as directly affecting their own everyday lives. What attracted me to the Social Democrat Group was their belief that we should focus on the everyday concerns that most people in the country have, that is, the need for better health services, education and transport links, as well as better-quality, well-paid jobs. For the party to recover nationally, especially if we are going to be more than just a party for affluent Remain-voting suburbs in the South-East, we need a broad appeal. I believe the Social Democrat Group, with its emphasis on down-to-earth bread-and-butter issues, shows the way for how our party can become a truly national party, speaking up for the disadvantaged as well as the well-off in society.

Deborah Newton-Cook – Executive member

As a student, I was looking for a pro-European party that would welcome young women who hoped to get into politics one day. Then, in 1981, the SDP was launched.

Roy Jenkins had been our European Commissioner and Shirley Williams was championing more women in politics. It was radical, pro-European and had a social democratic agenda. I had found my political home.

Zip forward to 2020 and I am still here in the Liberal Democrats. The 1988 merger of the SDP and Liberal Party was the year that I started a career in EU public affairs in Brussels. My party is still passionately pro-European but often concentrates more on the 'liberal' aspects of our policies than the 'social democrat' ones. We need to put the people who are at the bottom of society to the forefront.

I joined the Social Democrat Group just as the party has elected a leader who puts a very high priority on caring for carers. The September 2020 Party Conference also supported a universal basic income for all adults. So, perhaps social democracy is already having a revival! I hope to write contributions on a regular basis, and debate radical ideas. We need to be a radical party that appeals to voters who are truly fed up with both the Labour and Conservative Parties.

Tim Caswell – Executive member

A book on the future of social democracy begs the question: what do we mean by social democracy in the 21st century? Based on our history, I have attempted a definition that must be adapted as we face the challenge of shaping the future together.

Social democracy is the belief that neither the free market nor state ownership can achieve a society in which the economy works for everyone. Social democrats believe that rational evidence-based policy, a mixed economy, international cooperation, enhanced democracy, a positive role for the state, environmental sustainability and greater equality are the foundations of a prosperous and fair society. We believe that the rights we enjoy are balanced by the responsibilities we owe each other and value negative and positive freedom equally.

Rhi Jones – Executive member

The Social Democrat Group matters because it gives voice to the need to tackle social justice and reduce poverty within the Liberal Democrats. Through conference events, articles, the newsletter and now this book, the group challenges the party to focus on the concerns of most voters, and particularly women, around the lack of housing availability, low pay, job insecurity and the continued reduction in social provisions. It is clear that the economic impacts of COVID-19 have hit women hardest in our society and we need to be their voice.

Our society is so unequal and unfair, so it is vital to start tackling this now. I hope this book will help in that endeavour.

Rob Jackson – Treasurer

I joined the Liberal Democrats in 2015 after many years as a Labour member. At the time, the Labour Party seemed to be moving to the left (as it definitely did under Jeremy Corbyn). I felt that there was no longer a home for a Social Democrat like myself there. In joining the Liberal Democrats, I hoped to find other social democrats, and saw a post by George Kendall on Liberal Democrat Voice shortly after joining. So, after discussions, we set up the Social Democrat Group. The group had a fairly quiet start but is now getting more members and will, I hope, help to encourage a revival of the social democrat tradition in the party going forwards.

David McKenzie – Executive member

I felt compelled to join the Social Democrat Group due to my own lived experiences of politics. I was lucky enough to grow up under the progressive agenda of both New Labour and the Lib–Lab government in Scotland; Greenock, my hometown, had suffered a substantial level of industrial decline from the 1980s onwards and had a number of difficult social issues.

After over a decade spent in the Labour Party, I joined the Liberal Democrats in 2019. The Social Democrat Group exists to rightly link our heritage to the legacy of the SDP and the great reforming tradition of post-war Britain. We exist to cultivate an intellectual ecosystem on the progressive Left that generates radical ideas for social reform.

Too often do I see our politics regress, where children growing up will have suffered a worse degree of social and economic issues than I did. It is our duty to offer a pragmatic programme of government based on the principles of social democracy, tackling the five giants on the road of reconstruction: Want, Disease, Ignorance, Squalor and Idleness.

Index